700+ VERBAL EN

and how to use them in your writing

AN EXPERIMENTAL PLAY ON WORDS

with Laura Grebe and Reji Laberje

Quantity order requests can be emailed to:
publishing@rejilaberje.com

Or mailed to:
Reji Laberje Writing and Publishing
Publishing Orders
234 W. Broadway Street
Waukesha, WI 53186

Grebe, Laura
700+ Verbal Emojis
Contributing Author: Reji Laberje
Contributing Editor: Reji Laberje
Cover Design: Michael Nicloy
Interior Layout: Reji Laberje

ISBN-10: 194590707X
ISBN-13: 978-1945907074

SALES Categories:
Reference / Writing, Research & Publishing Guides / Writing / Fiction
Humor & Entertainment / Humor / Puns & Wordplay
Reference / Dictionaries & Thesauruses / Synonyms & Antonyms

BISAC Codes:
LAN021000Language Arts & Disciplines / Vocabulary
LAN005000Language Arts & Disciplines / Composition & Creative Writing
HUM019000Humor / Topic / Language

Writing and Publishing
www.rejilaberje.com

Dedication

For my various relatives who like words. For Mom and Dad, and Jeannie for complaining about thesauruses since the day I was born. And for Angela and Reji who looked at a random list of words I made for myself and saw the makings of this.

Verbal Emojis

Verbal Emojis

Verbal Emojis

VERBAL

Emojis

Verbal

Emojis

VERBAL

Emojis

Foreword

"How are you today?"

"Fine."

At least, that's the answer 99.9999999% (...99.999999999999999%) of us would give. Whether it's your best friend, your spouse, a co-worker, the cashier at the grocery store, or the stranger you pass at the park on a walk.

*But are we really? Is anyone really just fine? ....Are you? Are you really just **fine**?*

I'm not sure if the reason people answer fine is because they can't find a word suitable enough and don't want to have to go through a whole explanation to get there, or if we just don't want to let people know how we really feel.

I have found myself at the receiving end of this question and found myself answering "fine" for both reasons. Sometimes, I just don't have the words to express how I'm feeling.

"I'm fine. My baby was up all night for the third night in a row and I'm exhausted but I love snuggling with her in the dark when it's just us and it's so quiet and she looks at me with her big blue eyes and I can just hug her and love her up. It makes for long days, and I'm low on energy. But I love it and wouldn't have it any other way. So, yes. I'm fine."

And sometimes I just don't want people to know for whatever reason. They don't really care anyway, right? They are saying "How are you?" with the same expectation as "Hello." It is merely a greeting. Do I really want to bother them with how I actually feel? Do they deserve to be privy to my life right now? Do I tell the truth? Do I lie? I lie. "Fine."

Either way, we are not doing ourselves justice. You know the saying "fake it until you make it"? Say "fine" enough and you'll convince yourself that everything is fine. Even when it's not. Even when it's so far from fine. Even when it's so much greater than fine!

*As an experiment, I decided to actually track how I was feeling on certain days. I considered it an experiment of honesty with myself. I discovered that I felt everything . . . everything **but** fine. Sure, I was fine on some days and in some ways. But overall, I wasn't fine. I don't mean I was always sad, or disappointed, or below fine. Some days I was excited, peppy, jovial...even kinky....*

Because I'm a list person, I made a list of all the different feelings I had (well, at least those I remembered to record) over an identifiable interval of, say, nine months, and let me tell you; I felt a lot more than just . . . fine.

~Laura

About this Book

Laura works with Reji Laberje Writing and Publishing for her Experimental Word Play books and other publications.

We have an awesome online place with cool stuff . . . video, audio, downloadables and social media mayhem. You can learn about Laura, her books, really wicked awesome stuff like these lists, and so much more!

We call it her "Electronic Resource Hub", or, ERH.

I personally can't wait to see what happens. Laura's like our own personal grammar girl . . . but with word banks – Word Girl!

In fact, if you check back, and back, and back, we'll be adding, and adding, and adding to it. You'll find—not just really cool Experimental Word Play stuff from "Happenings", "Verbal Emojis", and "Still Useful Words", but also her upcoming "Cupcake Therapy" book, a maternity journal like no other, and eventually books ranging from children's mysteries to Patent Law?

Yeah.
We know.
She's pretty flipping impressive.
We love her, too!

At any rate, you can visit Laura Grebe's ERH by scanning the code below with your smart device or typing in the website on your chosen browser. Check out all those cool ERH goodies and a bunch of other useful knowledge on her publisher's site.

When you do give in to the digital peer pressure, we say "Thanks", "Merci", "Gracias", and—of course—"Danke" for dropping by!

Yours in writing,
Reji Laberje and Laura's Publishing Team!

Laura Grebe – Electronic Resource Hub

www.rejilaberje.com/laura-grebe.html

"For your born writer, nothing is so healing as the realization that he has come upon the right word."

~ *Catherine Drinker Bowen*

List

VERBAL

List

VERBAL

Emojis

Verbal

Emojis

List
Emojis

Verbal Emojis List

Do you remember a while back when Facebook launched its "hover over for additional reactions" feature? People complained that "thumbs up" wasn't adequate for reacting to people's posts. Nobody wanted to "LIKE" the fact that somebody's Grandmother passed away, but - in the same post, they did desire to like the request for prayers. Enter the sad face. So now you can select from a bunch of emojis. There's a heart, laughing face, crying face, shocked face, and an angry face. Now, for Grandmum's passing, we can display a . . . crying face (which I've also seen mistaken for a sweating face, by the way).

The selection of emojis for texting is also increasing. In fact, just a quick search of the app store gives me 500+ results for emoji apps and add-ons, each boasting their numbers of hundreds and thousands of emojis because it's not enough that you share a sad face, you want a sad face . . . on a cat (this is the internet, after all).

All of these emojis just to express how someone is feeling in a single character.

What happens when you can't use a character? And is a character really enough, anyway? In overwhelm, we find ourselves back at "how are you?" and "fine."

The following is a list of over 700 words and phrases (704, to be exact) to express how someone feels. Consider these your **verbal emojis**—*the long form of those single character emotions. Verbal emojis are great for expressing a character's feelings, state of mind, reaction, or environment. Verbal emojis can be used to further define a character and help a reader empathize with a character. Verbal emojis create deep and complex characters.*

Verbal emojis are also perfect to use in writing because, well.....they are WORDS! Whoda thunk?

Also great for educators and counselors, I hope you'll enjoy this step beyond thumbs up, heart, laughing, crying, and shocked in the experimental play on words, "700+ Verbal Emojis".

1.	Abnormous	45.	Astonishing
2.	Absent	46.	Astounded
3.	Absorbed	47.	Astounding
4.	Absorbing	48.	Attentive
5.	Absurd	49.	Attractive
6.	Achy	50.	Audacious
7.	Active	51.	Avid
8.	Admired	52.	Awake
9.	Adorable	53.	Awakened
10.	Adored	54.	Aware
11.	Adrift	55.	Awed
12.	Adroit	56.	Awe-inspiring
13.	Adventurous	57.	Awesome
14.	Affectionate	58.	Awkward
15.	Affirmed	59.	Bashful
16.	Affluent	60.	Beaten
17.	Aggressive	61.	Beautiful
18.	Agitated	62.	Behind
19.	Agreeable	63.	Beloved
20.	Ahead	64.	Besieged
21.	Alert	65.	Bewitching
22.	Alive	66.	Big
23.	Alluring	67.	Bitter
24.	Altruistic	68.	Blasé
25.	Amatory	69.	Blessed
26.	Amazed	70.	Blissful
27.	Amazing	71.	Bloated
28.	Ambitious	72.	Blue
29.	Angry	73.	Bogglish
30.	Animated	74.	Bold
31.	Annoyed	75.	Bored
32.	Anticipatory	76.	Boring
33.	Antiquated	77.	Bossy
34.	Antsy	78.	Bouncy
35.	Anxious	79.	Brainy
36.	Apathetic	80.	Brave
37.	Appreciated	81.	Breathtaking
38.	Appreciative	82.	Bright
39.	Apprehensive	83.	Brilliant
40.	Aroused	84.	Bubbly
41.	Articulate	85.	Bulging
42.	Artistic	86.	Busy
43.	Ashamed	87.	Calm
44.	Assiduous	88.	Candid

89.	Capable	133.	Creepy
90.	Carefree	134.	Crushed
91.	Caring	135.	Curvaceous
92.	Casual	136.	Cynical
93.	Certain	137.	Damaged
94.	Changing	138.	Daring
95.	Charmed	139.	Dazzling
96.	Charming	140.	Decisive
97.	Chaste	141.	Dehydrated
98.	Cheerful	142.	Dejected
99.	Cheery	143.	Delayed
100.	Cherished	144.	Delicate
101.	Chic	145.	Delighted
102.	Childish	146.	Dependable
103.	Claustrophobic	147.	Depleted
104.	Clean	148.	Depressed
105.	Clever	149.	Desired
106.	Clingy	150.	Desolate
107.	Closed	151.	Determined
108.	Cold	152.	Difficult
109.	Collected	153.	Diplomatic
110.	Colossal	154.	Disbelieving
111.	Comely	155.	Dissatisfied
112.	Comfortable	156.	Distended
113.	Comforting	157.	Distinctive
114.	Commendable	158.	Distracted
115.	Compassionate	159.	Distressed
116.	Complex	160.	Distrustful
117.	Complicated	161.	Disturbed
118.	Composed	162.	Dizzy
119.	Concerned	163.	Docile
120.	Confident	164.	Doubtful
121.	Confused	165.	Dowdy
122.	Constrained	166.	Down
123.	Consumed	167.	Drained
124.	Contemplative	168.	Dramatic
125.	Content	169.	Dreaming
126.	Cool	170.	Dreamy
127.	Courageous	171.	Driving
128.	Coveted	172.	Drowsy
129.	Cowardly	173.	Dry
130.	Cozy	174.	Dubious
131.	Crafty	175.	Dull
132.	Creative	176.	Eager

177.	Earnest	221.	Exquisite
178.	Easygoing	222.	Extraordinary
179.	Ebullient	223.	Extroverted
180.	Ecstatic	224.	Exultant
181.	Edgy	225.	Fabulous
182.	Effervescent	226.	Faint
183.	Egocentric	227.	Fake
184.	Egotistic	228.	Famous
185.	Embarrassed	229.	Fantastic
186.	Emotional	230.	Fascinated
187.	Empowered	231.	Fascinating
188.	Empowering	232.	Fashionable
189.	Empty	233.	Fat
190.	Encouraged	234.	Fatigued
191.	Encouraging	235.	Favored
192.	Energized	236.	Fearful
193.	Engaged	237.	Fearless
194.	Engorged	238.	Feeble
195.	Engrossed	239.	Fervent
196.	Enjoyable	240.	Fiery
197.	Enlivened	241.	Fine
198.	Enraged	242.	Firm
199.	Enthralling	243.	Flabbergasted
200.	Enthusiastic	244.	Flattered
201.	Enticing	245.	Floppy
202.	Equipped	246.	Flummoxed
203.	Erotic	247.	Flushed
204.	Erratic	248.	Focused
205.	Esteemed	249.	Foggy
206.	Estimable	250.	Foreign
207.	Estranged	251.	Forgetful
208.	Evolving	252.	Forlorn
209.	Exalted	253.	Fortunate
210.	Excellent	254.	Fragile
211.	Exceptional	255.	Frail
212.	Excited	256.	Frantic
213.	Exhausted	257.	Fraught
214.	Expanded	258.	Frazzled
215.	Expanding	259.	Free
216.	Expectant	260.	Fresh
217.	Experienced	261.	Friendly
218.	Explosive	262.	Frightened
219.	Exposed	263.	Frisky
220.	Expressive	264.	Fulfilled

265.	Full	309.	Hurt
266.	Functional	310.	Ideal
267.	Funny	311.	Ill
268.	Generous	312.	Illecebrous
269.	Gentle	313.	Illogical
270.	Gigantic	314.	Immature
271.	Glad	315.	Impatient
272.	Gloomy	316.	Imperfect
273.	Glum	317.	Imperious
274.	Gorgeous	318.	Impious
275.	Grand	319.	Impish
276.	Grateful	320.	Important
277.	Gratified	321.	Impressed
278.	Great	322.	Impressive
279.	Greedy	323.	Impulsive
280.	Groggy	324.	Incredible
281.	Growing	325.	Indecisive
282.	Guilty	326.	Inflated
283.	Gutsy	327.	Influential
284.	Hairy	328.	Infuriated
285.	Happy	329.	Inquisitive
286.	Hardened	330.	Insane
287.	Hard-working	331.	Insecure
288.	Harmless	332.	Insignificant
289.	Hassled	333.	Insistent
290.	Haunted	334.	Insomniatic
291.	Heavy	335.	Inspired
292.	Heroic	336.	Inspiring
293.	Hesitant	337.	Instinctive
294.	Hidden	338.	Intelligent
295.	Hilarious	339.	Interested
296.	Hip	340.	Interesting
297.	Hollow	341.	Interrupted
298.	Honest	342.	Intrigued
299.	Honored	343.	Intriguing
300.	Hopeful	344.	Introverted
301.	Hormonal	345.	Intuitive
302.	Hot	346.	Inundated
303.	Hubristic	347.	Irksome
304.	Huge	348.	Irrational
305.	Humble	349.	Irreplaceable
306.	Hungry	350.	Irritable
307.	Hunted	351.	Itchy
308.	Hurried	352.	Jittery

353.	Jolly		397.	Mindful
354.	Jovial		398.	Miraculous
355.	Joyful		399.	Mischievous
356.	Joyous		400.	Miserable
357.	Judicious		401.	Misguided
358.	Keen		402.	Misjudged
359.	Kept		403.	Misunderstood
360.	Kind		404.	Modest
361.	Kindhearted		405.	Monstrous
362.	Lackadaisical		406.	Moody
363.	Lacking		407.	Morose
364.	Lamenting		408.	Motivated
365.	Late		409.	Mysterious
366.	Laudable		410.	Naïve
367.	Lazy		411.	Natural
368.	Lethargic		412.	Naughty
369.	Lewd		413.	Nauseous
370.	Lively		414.	Needed
371.	Livid		415.	Needy
372.	Logical		416.	Neglected
373.	Longing		417.	Nervous
374.	Loquacious		418.	Notable
375.	Lost		419.	Noticed
376.	Loved		420.	Oblivious
377.	Lovely		421.	Obtuse
378.	Loving		422.	Odd
379.	Lucky		423.	OK
380.	Magical		424.	Old
381.	Majestic		425.	Open
382.	Marginalized		426.	Ordinary
383.	Marked		427.	Organized
384.	Marvelous		428.	Orgasmic
385.	Massive		429.	Outgoing
386.	Matchless		430.	Outspoken
387.	Mature		431.	Outstanding
388.	Mediocre		432.	Overawed
389.	Meditative		433.	Overcome
390.	Meek		434.	Overextended
391.	Mellow		435.	Overwhelmed
392.	Memorable		436.	Overwhelming
393.	Mesmerizing		437.	Parched
394.	Messy		438.	Particular
395.	Methodical		439.	Passionate
396.	Mind-blowing		440.	Pathetic

441.	Patient	485.	Randy
442.	Peaceful	486.	Rare
443.	Peachy	487.	Rational
444.	Peppy	488.	Ravenous
445.	Perceptive	489.	Ready
446.	Perfect	490.	Receptive
447.	Perplexed	491.	Recognizable
448.	Persevering	492.	Refreshed
449.	Persistent	493.	Regretful
450.	Phenomenal	494.	Rejuvenated
451.	Picky	495.	Relaxed
452.	Pious	496.	Reliable
453.	Playful	497.	Relieved
454.	Pleased	498.	Relished
455.	Plucky	499.	Remarkable
456.	Poised	500.	Renewed
457.	Poor	501.	Resigned
458.	Positive	502.	Resolute
459.	Powerful	503.	Respected
460.	Practical	504.	Responsive
461.	Praiseworthy	505.	Rested
462.	Prayerful	506.	Restful
463.	Precious	507.	Revived
464.	Precious	508.	Rewarded
465.	Predictable	509.	Rich
466.	Preoccupied	510.	Risky
467.	Prepared	511.	Riveted
468.	Primed	512.	Riveting
469.	Privileged	513.	Rude
470.	Prized	514.	Ruffled
471.	Protected	515.	Rushed
472.	Protective	516.	Sacred
473.	Proud	517.	Sad
474.	Puffy	518.	Safe
475.	Purposeful	519.	Sagacious
476.	Pushy	520.	Sane
477.	Puzzled	521.	Sarcastic
478.	Puzzling	522.	Sassy
479.	Queasy	523.	Satisfied
480.	Querulous	524.	Scared
481.	Questioning	525.	Scarred
482.	Quick	526.	Scrawny
483.	Quiet	527.	Secure
484.	Racy	528.	Seeking

529.	Seen	573.	Stationary
530.	Selfish	574.	Steadfast
531.	Selfless	575.	Stiff
532.	Sensational	576.	Still
533.	Sensible	577.	Stimulated
534.	Sensitive	578.	Stinky
535.	Sensual	579.	Stirred
536.	Set	580.	Strained
537.	Sexy	581.	Strange
538.	Shaky	582.	Stressed
539.	Sharp	583.	Stretched
540.	Sheltered	584.	Striving
541.	Shining	585.	Strong
542.	Shiny	586.	Strong-minded
543.	Short-tempered	587.	Stubborn
544.	Shrewd	588.	Stuck
545.	Shy	589.	Stuffed
546.	Sick	590.	Stunning
547.	Significant	591.	Stylish
548.	Silent	592.	Suggestive
549.	Simple	593.	Sulky
550.	Sleepy	594.	Super
551.	Sluggish	595.	Superb
552.	Small	596.	Superior
553.	Smart	597.	Supported
554.	Smiley	598.	Supportive
555.	Smooth	599.	Surprised
556.	Smug	600.	Surprising
557.	Snug	601.	Surrendered
558.	Sophisticated	602.	Suspicious
559.	Sore	603.	Swamped
560.	Sorrowful	604.	Sweet
561.	Sought	605.	Swollen
562.	Special	606.	Sympathetic
563.	Speechless	607.	Taciturn
564.	Spent	608.	Targeted
565.	Spicy	609.	Taxed
566.	Spirited	610.	Temperamental
567.	Splendid	611.	Tenacious
568.	Spontaneous	612.	Tender
569.	Stable	613.	Tense
570.	Stagnant	614.	Terrific
571.	Starving	615.	Thankful
572.	Static	616.	Thirsty

617.	Thoughtful	661.	Unsteady
618.	Thrilled	662.	Unsure
619.	Tight	663.	Untiring
620.	Timely	664.	Unwanted
621.	Timid	665.	Unwearied
622.	Tired	666.	Upset
623.	Toasted	667.	Used
624.	Toasty	668.	Useful
625.	Touching	669.	Valiant
626.	Tranquil	670.	Valuable
627.	Transfixed	671.	Vehement
628.	Transformed	672.	Victorious
629.	Transforming	673.	Vigilant
630.	Transparent	674.	Virtuous
631.	Traumatized	675.	Vital
632.	Treasured	676.	Vivacious
633.	Tremendous	677.	Volatile
634.	Trendy	678.	Voracious
635.	Troubled	679.	Vulnerable
636.	Trusted	680.	Wanted
637.	Trustful	681.	Wanting
638.	Trusting	682.	Warm
639.	Trustworthy	683.	Watchful
640.	Turgid	684.	Weak
641.	Unbelievable	685.	Weary
642.	Uncertain	686.	Wise
643.	Unchanging	687.	Wistful
644.	Uncomfortable	688.	Withdrawn
645.	Understood	689.	Withered
646.	Undervalued	690.	Woeful
647.	Undisturbed	691.	Wonderful
648.	Uneasy	692.	Woozy
649.	Unfocused	693.	Wordy
650.	Unhappy	694.	Worldly
651.	Unimportant	695.	Worn
652.	Unique	696.	Worried
653.	Unpredictable	697.	Worthwhile
654.	Unprepared	698.	Worthy
655.	Unrecognizable	699.	Wounded
656.	Unrelenting	700.	Wowed
657.	Unruffled	701.	Wretched
658.	Unsettled	702.	Yearning
659.	Unshakable	703.	Young
660.	Unstable	704.	Zealous

Word

Word Play!

Play

Word Play!

Word

Play

Play

Word

WORD PLAY!

WORD PLAY . . . YOUR Verbal Emojis List

So, how exactly ARE you feeling? In this moment, if you had to pick one word or phrase to describe your sentiment, your emotion, your verbal emoji, what would it be? Did we cover it? Even writing these, more came to mind; I'm sure the same is true for you in reading them (or, more likely, scanning them). Let those 704 verbal emojis be just the beginning and choose to add your own below!

705. _____

706. _____

707. _____

708. _____

709. _____

710. _____

711. _____

712. _____

713. _____

714. _____

715. _____

716. _____

717. _____

718. _____

719. _____

720. _____

721. _____

722. _____

723. _____

724. _____

725. _____

726. _____

727. _____

728. _____

729. _____

730. _____

731. _____

732. _____

733. _____

734. _____

735. _____

736. _____

737. _____

738. _____

739. _____

740. _____

741. _____

742. _____

743. _____

744. _____

Need more room? Really? Well, now you're just showing off! It's all good, though. I left blank and lined pages at the back of the book for the overachievers just like you! Phhhttt!

Dictionary

Dictionary

VERBAL EMOJIS

Thesaurus

Dictionary

Verbal Emojis

Thesaurus

VERBAL EMOJIS

Thesaurus

15

Verbal Emojis Dictionary and Thesaurus

I'm sure some of you were doing a little sigh of relief when you saw the words "dictionary" and "thesaurus." The rest of you already pulled out a dictionary or thesaurus out and looked up some of those words.

Let's face it. With the age of emojis, who verbalizes how they feel anymore? Who really says anything beyond the socially acceptable "fine"?

Writers. That's who. As writers, we are forced to use verbal emojis because a page filled with little yellow faces would just be weird. And cryptic. And a bit awkward.

Sure, your character may be happy, but would you put a ☺ in the middle of your beautifully written narrative? You know, like I just did right there? Would your character even use the word happy? Maybe yes. Maybe no. If maybe no, we hope we got you covered. Because now you can go to "happy" (yup, we're alphabetical again), and find other words that mean "happy" other than..."happy," I guess.

*Don't let your character suffer by choosing verbal emojis that your character would not use. Out of the now expanded listing of over 700 words, there's got to be one that's suitable for **your** character's personality.*

These definitions, and some synonymous words, were derived from exchanges between professional authors after consulting the Merriam Webster Dictionary, Oxford English Dictionary, Dictionary.com, the Urban Dictionary (online), Roget's Thesaurus, and Thesaurus.com.

In short, I've got you a writer's dictionary and thesaurus of verbal emojis, here. It's in alphabetical order once again because is there really any other way to organize verbal emojis, anyway?

...oh wait. There might be. But I won't go into details here. Spoilers!

Anyway, here it comes — the dictionary and thesaurus of verbal emojis according to an Experimental Word Player . . . sweet!

Word or Phrase	Definition and Synonyms
Abnormous	As it sounds – part "abnormal" and part "enormous", abnormally large, or enormously out of the ordinary
Absent	Gone, not present, unavailable emotionally or physically
Absorbed	Fully consumed, preoccupied, or engaged
Absorbing	In the activity of becoming captivated or intrigued
Absurd	Goofy, out of norms, illogical, and ludicrous
Achy	A feeling of being sore, weak, and run-down
Active	Moving, busy, or athletic are each active to various degrees; check out temperances, later!
Admired	What we feel for Lin Manuel Miranda, JK Rowling, George Washington, Winston Churchill, and Jesus, all for very different reasons. Also to feel respected, worshipped, or even glorified.
Adorable	So stinkin' cute! A-dork-able! Bloody cheek-pinchable!
Adored	To be cherished, loved, and desired in a positive, loving manner
Adrift	Lost, wandering, and purposeless
Adroit	Smart, but the kind of smart you would associate with the greatest BBC sleuths; cunning, clever, and sharp-witted
Adventurous	Up-for-anything, desirous of adrenaline-inducing activities, open-minded
Affectionate	Cuddly, joined, close, and horny . . . dependent upon the extremity
Affirmed	A feeling of self-confidence and assuredness, feeling proven
Affluent	Advanced in prosperity of all kinds from health to wealth, also rich, famous, or influential
Aggressive	Not the "passive" kind – that just sucks; but the "go get 'em tiger!" kind, being boldly and unashamedly driven
Agitated	Also irritated, annoyed, and frustrated
Agreeable	People-pleasing, carefree, and easy-going with regard to most decisions
Ahead	On top of things, leading, and making paths
Alert	Just a 5-Hour Energy® shot away; also your three-month old at 3:00 in the morning, awake, focused, and unwavering
Alive	Breathing and beating (your heart, not others); also a general feeling of exhilaration
Alluring	Seductive, "Why don't you come on up and see me?" ~Mae West
Altruistic	Philanthropic, giving, Christian, self-sacrificing
Amatory	Passionately loving, feverish with desire
Amazed	Shocked, surprised, truly caught "off-guard"
Amazing	To feel proud, blown away with positivity, on top of the world
Ambitious	Driven, motivated, inspired, and on your way
Angry	Mad, hot under the collar, and rabid
Animated	Bright, lively (ironically, since animation is actually the opposite of live), and expressive

Annoyed	Frustrated, irritated, agitated
Anticipatory	Impatient (maybe), anxious, in-wait
Antiquated	As a person, to feel old, out-of-date, or expired (You're not. See "Worthy".)
Antsy	Nervously anxious, jittery with impatience
Anxious	Worried or preoccupied about what is to come for you or a loved one, impatient
Apathetic	Do you really even care what this word means?
Appreciated	Loved, looked up to, respected, value
Appreciative	Feeling gratitude, respect, and value for another
Apprehensive	Nervous, unsure, indecisive
Aroused	Piqued, interested, amatory
Articulate	Specific, intellectual, wordy
Artistic	Creative, imaginative, cultured
Ashamed	Embarrassed, worried about others' opinions, guilty
Assiduous	Unstoppable, diligent, untiring
Astonishing	Amazing, incredible, unbelievable
Astounded	To be dumbfounded by another's amazing, incredible, unbelievable acts
Astounding	Surprise to a confusing and confounding level
Attentive	To be mindful and focused
Attractive	Beautiful, stunning, lovely, hot, gorgeous, and striking . . . and of which adjectives will do more to make a wife amatory than looking "nice"
Audacious	Gutsy, boldly righteous, stubbornly confident
Avid	Experienced, well-trained, successful
Awake	Wide-eyed, caffeinated . . . hold on; getting a coffee warm-up – feel free to join me . . .
Awakened	. . . sip, ahh . . . and now? I'm awakened – made alert – by the coffee, but sometimes by the crying child at 3:00 A.M. and other times by the alarm six or seven times or however many more I decide to hit the snooze
Aware	Knowing, with full understanding, eyes wide open
Awed	Humbled by beauty, power, or acts of greatness
Awe-inspiring	Moved to make a difference as a result of the humbling beauty, power, or act of greatness
Awesome	At one time, this was to be full of awe (replacing the awful which, over time, became negative), but it now is on par with cool, nifty, groovy, and other generational slang to mean that something is great . . . just great (but, without the sarcasm)
Awkward	Uncomfortable like your mother sitting on your father's lap or the woman nursing her child who just started t-ball
Bashful	Shy, reserved, quiet
Beaten	Defeated, crushed, disheartened, giving up
Beautiful	See "attractive"

Behind	Negatively can be a feeling of overwhelm, lacking, and procrastination's result, but can be positive if it's the feeling of another BEHIND you, supporting you, lifting you up, and taking your side in a difficult time
Beloved	Adored, cherished, held in honor
Besieged	Attacked, cornered, trapped
Bewitching	Entrancing, captivating to others, spellbinding
Big	Abnormous, huge, waddling, large, growing
Bitter	Angry, jaded, unforgiving, stiff
Blasé	Bored, uncaring, disconnected
Blessed	Honored, joyful, filled with gratitude
Blissful	Exuberant joy, afterglow, light happiness
Bloated	Fat, full, stuffed
Blue	Sad, down, melancholy
Bogglish	Unconvinced, skeptical, leery
Bold	Daring, courageous, assertive
Bored	Uninterested, lost, pointless
Boring	To be the cause (whether true or not) of a lost feeling, pointlessness, or disinterest of others
Bossy	"Do it my way! My way is the ONLY way!" ~Bossy McBossypants
Bouncy	Light, youthful, energized
Brainy	Smart, intelligent, witty, clever
Brave	Daring, courageous, heroic, and also the wild redheaded bear tamer in all of us
Breathtaking	Ooh! This one! Add this one to the "attractive" list, too; score points
Bright	A light, happy, positive person, Pollyannaish, to the greatest generation
Brilliant	Smart in a puzzle-solving manner; intelligent and clever together to accomplish great things
Bubbly	Bouncy, except a bit ditzy (unless you're a toddler, then you can be bubbly all you want without being ditzy)
Bulging	Awkwardly large, misshapen, oversized
Busy	Chaotic, overwhelmed, and the only word catching up to "Fine" as the western world's answer to "How are you?"
Calm	Peaceful, still, unworried, and surrendered; the embodiment of the serenity prayer
Candid	Honest, sometimes brutally so, frank, and blunt
Capable	Strong and able, experienced, trained, and prepared
Carefree	Unscheduled, unattached, and—about at least daily stresses— uncaring
Caring	Thoughtful of and maternal for the well-being of others
Casual	Informal, laid back, loose, and friendly – usually as a result of a welcoming family or friend-filled environment

Certain	Sure, confident, undoubting of a thought, feeling, or opinion
Changing	In transition, in flux, the most unsure time of all, usually in wait for something or someone, perhaps even a new you
Charmed	To be delighted by flattery, though not necessarily of the romantic kind
Charming	As in, Prince; as in, the embodiment of charm toward others
Chaste	Virgin, pure and true
Cheerful	Literally full of cheer, to be happy enough inside that it flows out, too
Cheery	To have a pleasant or joyful disposition
Cherished	Adored, loved, honored, and respected
Chic	Trendy, en vogue, stylish
Childish	Immature, whiny, and irresponsible (unlike child-like which is innocent, naïve, and youthful)
Claustrophobic	Nervous particularly as a result of tight spaces or closing crowds
Clean	Fresh, washed, and fragrant
Clever	Witty, sleuth-like, and . . . oh yeah . . . The Doctor, of course – clever boy
Clingy	Protective, attached, often as a result of preoccupation rather than affection
Closed	Stubborn, unbending, unwilling to share, care, or connect
Cold	Snobbish, aloof, indifferent, and thoughtless; from Hans Christian Anderson's "The Snow Queen" originally which is a much darker story than its modern sister, "Frozen"
Collected	Together, composed, organized in thought and heart
Colossal	Enormous in physical, emotional, spiritual, or conceptual manner, larger than life, and enormously insurmountable
Comely	Beautiful or handsome, for women, often refers to voluptuousness of physique
Comfortable	Lazy, unstressed, relaxed
Comforting	Emotionally giving, supportive, and empathetic
Commendable	Admirable, honorable, and respectable usually as the result of an act of goodness or kindness
Compassionate	Sympathy backed up with action, care that drives motivation toward change and positive acts
Complex	Confusing, intricately designed, puzzling
Complicated	Difficult, confusing, and confounding
Composed	See "collected"
Concerned	Worried, preoccupied, and ruminating
Confident	Self-assured, undoubting, and possibly, dependent upon the temperance, egotistical or arrogant (getting interested in that temperance section, yet?)
Confused	Uncertain of answers, puzzled, confounded
Constrained	Held back, reserved by others, unable to be one's self

Consumed	Fully lost in mind, body, and spirit over a specific thing or person
Contemplative	Deep in thought over results of different decisions, thoughtful, methodical
Content	Happy, satisfied, and accepting of joy
Cool	Can be a feeling of "chic-ness" or one of being aloof and disconnected
Courageous	Brave and steady, heroic
Coveted	Desired, wanted, lusted for
Cowardly	Yellow (does anybody say that, anymore?)
Cozy	Comfortable, warm, and close, with a loving overtone
Crafty	Witty and sneaky or, in a more traditional usage, artistic and creative
Creative	Artistic, imaginative, crafty
Creepy	Sneaky, slimy, and dirty
Crushed	Defeated, beaten, deflated, and submissive
Curvaceous	Voluptuous, shapely, and buxom, from Betty Boop to Marilyn Monroe to Scarlet Johanson, curves will always have representation
Cynical	Skeptical, unbelieving, and stubborn in faith
Damaged	Jaded, broken-spirited, victimized, or abused . . . some have it done to them and others do it to themselves, but all are worthy of fixing
Daring	Adventurous, risk-taking, and brave
Dazzling	Sparkling, glowing, and beautiful
Decisive	Forceful alpha, dominant, and steady
Dehydrated	Parched, thirsty, dry
Dejected	Discouraged, deflated, uninspired, lost, and broken
Delayed	Late, tardy, behind
Delicate	Fragile and flower-like, but of fine workmanship – don't underestimate the delicate
Delighted	Pleased and full of joy as a result of something that occurred or will occur
Dependable	Reliable, responsible, mature, and accountable
Depleted	Your grocery budget, due to diapers, in the first month of a baby's life
Depressed	Physiological mental sadness, melancholy, clinically blue
Desired	Lusted for, wanted
Desolate	Lonely, set-apart, left behind
Determined	Focused, driven, and seeking a result
Difficult	Stubborn, demanding, and troublesome
Diplomatic	Almost every consolation speech ever given in the history of American politics; Kindly communicating unkind sentiments
Disbelieving	Skeptical, cynical, faithless
Dissatisfied	Unhappy, discontented, and . . . left wanting

Distended	Stretched to maximum, bulging, and big to the point of tearing (or at least it seems that way)
Distinctive	Unique, individual, and special
Distracted	Inattentive, wandering mind, lost in thought, not present
Distressed	Stressed for negative reasons, preoccupied, ill with worry
Distrustful	Stand-offish, cautious, once-bitten twice-shy
Disturbed	Unsettled, upset, nauseous with disgust
Dizzy	Woozy, imbalanced, and faint-feeing
Docile	Lazy, still, submissive, and weak – negative connotation to the positive agreeable
Doubtful	Untrusting, skeptical, and cynical
Dowdy	Out-of-date, but also homely, sloppy, and ill-fitted to one's clothing, crowd, or situation
Down	Depressed, sad, melancholy, and blue
Drained	Exhausted, tired, spent
Dramatic	Over-emotional, angsty, over-the-top
Dreaming	Distracted, wandering mind, imagining
Dreamy	Idealistic, drifting, musing
Driving	Motivating, inspiring, pushing toward goals
Drowsy	Sleepy, fading, drifting
Dry	Parched, hard, flaky
Dubious	Doubtful, unbelievable, not likely
Dull	"Bueller. Bueller. Bueller." Ben Stein in "Ferris Bueller's Day Off" was the living exemplification of DULL . . . (intentionally, the "real" Ben Stein is rather funny)
Eager	Excited, looking forward to something with energy; eager beaver
Earnest	There's an importance to being this honest, diligent, and purpose-driven being
Easygoing	Laid back, agreeable, carefree
Ebullient	Lively, vivacious, and energetically excited
Ecstatic	Thrilled, jumpily excited
Edgy	Risk-taking, against the grain/norm, and irreverent
Effervescent	Bubbly, light, and joyful
Egocentric	Self-centered, self-serving, and conceited
Egotistic	Arrogant, pompous, and—also—egotistical (above)
Embarrassed	Ashamed, guilty, flustered
Emotional	Dramatic, sensitive, feeling
Empowered	Confident, inspired, driven by something or someone, usually toward the accomplishment of a goal
Empowering	To BE inspiring, motivating, and strengthening for others
Empty	Drained, lost, deflated, and purposeless or spiritless
Encouraged	To feel lifted up by others
Encouraging	To lift others up
Energized	Alert, motivated, and ready to face the world

Engaged	To be committed to something or someone in a deep connection or through a strong promise
Engorged	Bursting, popping . . . and FREAKING YUGE! (I just noticed I was feeling an awful lot of these while creating the Experimental Word Play series on bed rest during my pregnancy!)
Engrossed	Totally focused to complete lack of distraction.
Enjoyable	Fun to be around, fun to do things with, contented with the happiness one brings
Enlivened	See "Alert" and "Alive"
Enraged	Bloody, frothing MAD!
Enthralling	Positively engaging through distinctive qualities
Enthusiastic	Anticipated joy expressed early
Enticing	Teasing, alluring, seducing . . . though, it could also apply to the things done to reach enticement including attire, foods, etc.
Equipped	Prepared, ready; "God doesn't call the equipped; he equips the called." ~Rick Yancey
Erotic	Turned on, seductive, and alluring with filthy overtones . . . get your mind out of the gutter!
Erratic	Unpredictable, all over the place, meandering on physical, mental, emotional, or spiritual paths
Esteemed	Valued, respected, honored
Estimable	Praised, valued, and commendable
Estranged	Set apart, damaged, broken, lost
Evolving	Changing, morphing, growing, and—hopefully, advancing
Exalted	Raised, worshipped, glorified
Excellent	Bill and Ted's Adventure
Exceptional	Top-notch, cream-of-the-crop, the best of the best in excellence
Excited	Enthused, anticipatory, forward-looking, optimistic
Exhausted	Tired, drained, drowsy
Expanded	Grown, blown up
Expanding	Growing, widening
Expectant	Waiting with hope, anticipation (usually positive)
Experienced	Prepared, trained, and ready for specific tasks
Explosive	Boiling, raging, building
Exposed	Vulnerable, naked, on-display
Expressive	Animated, emotional, lit up
Exquisite	Yes! Add it to the list, boys! See "attractive" and let your list grow
Extraordinary	Brilliant, literally above or beyond ordinary
Extroverted	Outspoken, gregarious
Exultant	Triumphant, victorious, reveling
Fabulous	Fantastic, wonderful, amazing, and perfect
Faint	Weak-kneed, light-headed, dizzy, woozy
Fake	Two-faced

Famous	Known, center of attention, big fish
Fantastic	Glorious, fabulous, wonderful, amazing
Fascinated	Blown away, intrigued, interested
Fascinating	To be the source of blowing away, intriguing, and piquing interest
Fashionable	Chic, trendy, stylish, appealing (ooh! Add that last one to THE list)
Fat	Ab-freaking-normous, okay!
Fatigued	Tired, exhausted, drained, drowsy, wiped out
Favored	Highly favored, that is, and richly blessed
Fearful	Afraid, worrisome, frightened, preoccupied
Fearless	Adventurous, daring, bodacious, cocky
Feeble	Weak, meek, and small
Fervent	Passionate, driven, motivated, and hot
Fiery	Hot, turned on, passionate, (or possibly raging, mad, and angry)
Fine	Well, technically, this one can go on THE list, too, but let's assume this is the *other* "fine" and therefore should be avoided and replaced with another verbal emoji because, as we discussed, FINE usually isn't
Firm	Stubborn, unbending, stiff
Flabbergasted	Confounded, discombobulated, and metagrobolized because why not?
Flattered	Admired, complimented, stroked
Floppy	Droopy, limp, and deflated
Flummoxed	Confused, perplexed, stumped
Flushed	Blushing, rosy, glowing, ruddy
Focused	Engaged, absorbed, indistractable (sure. Why not?)
Foggy	Cloudy, visionless, directionless, unclear
Foreign	Wen rufst du ausländisch an?
Forgetful	I'm sorry, what?
Forlorn	Longing, yearning, and desiring
Fortunate	Blessed, grateful
Fragile	Delicate, damaged, or breakable, but also beautiful and light
Frail	Weak, fragile, and delicate
Frantic	Panicked, chaotic, bustling
Fraught	Laden, burdened, heavy
Frazzled	Frantic, unsteady, ragged
Free	Careless, unattached, empowered
Fresh	Ripe, healthy, clean
Friendly	Kind, nice (ugh! Nice is the twin to "fine" Forget I said that one)
Frightened	Fearful, afraid, worrisome, preoccupied
Frisky	Flirty, taunting, playful, teasing
Fulfilled	Blessed, purposeful, spirited
Full	All the time and yet never at all while pregnant

Functional	Working, practical, purposeful, and healthy (but, perhaps, barely in all of these cases)
Funny	Hilarious, giggly, and witty (to varying degrees)
Generous	Did you know that Denzel Washington, upon visiting a Fisher House (where family members of wounded veterans stay during their loved ones care at veteran's hospitals), asked "How much do one of these cost?" Upon hearing the price, he took out his checkbook and sponsored the full cost of the worthy cause. THAT is generous! So is giving, thoughtfulness, and a philanthropic heart
Gentle	Soft, calming, loving, and diplomatic in one's communications or presence
Gigantic	I think these words for big, enormous, and large are catching up to those for attractive!
Glad	Happy, joyful, contented, blessed, and blissful
Gloomy	Dark, depressed, melancholy, and pessimistic
Glum	Focusing on the negative, Debbie-Downer, Negative Nellie, etc.
Gorgeous	Okay . . . keep going. The race between abnormous and attractive is ON!
Grand	To feel important, larger than life, and respected (or, I guess, just big in a physical way, too)
Grateful	Blessed, appreciative, humbled
Gratified	To feel joy and satisfaction from being proven or accomplished at a task
Great	While possibly as dangerous as "fine", it can also be *genuinely* fantastic and wonderful
Greedy	Selfish, covetous, and fearful
Groggy	Sleepy, drowsy, foggy, and tired
Growing	Bulging and expanding physically or developing and maturing mentally, emotionally, professionally, or socially
Guilty	Ashamed, abashed
Gutsy	Brave, daring, and bold
Hairy	Fuzzy, nappy
Happy	Joyful, blissful, content, satisfied, blessed, and grateful
Hardened	Jaded, bitter, stiff, and unbending
Hard-working	Diligent, laborious, and dedicated
Harmless	Innocent, simple, and innocuous; "harmless as a fly"
Hassled	Bothered, annoyed, bugged
Haunted	Ghostly, bewitched, obsessed, or infested . . . SO? Who you gonna call?
Heavy	Burdened, laden, weighted or weighed down
Heroic	Courageous, selfless, outward-focused, brave
Hesitant	Pensive, unsure, or reluctant
Hidden	Incognito, invisible, or unknown
Hilarious	Funny, chuckle-inducing, and unpredictably tickled

Hip	In, chic, stylish, trendy, or fashionable, and—according to Huey Lewis—SQUARE!
Hollow	Empty, drained, vacuous, cavernous, holey (not Holy)
Honest	Truthful, veritable, and proven
Honored	Respected, admired, looked up to, and worshipped
Hopeful	Optimistic, idealistic, and forward-looking
Hormonal	Moody (usually), but also can refer to hot flashes (for women), water bloating, and yearnings (for men or women)
Hot	Sweating, sweltering, melting
Hubristic	Confident (bordering on cocky), self-assured, wise, and smart-alecky
Huge	Is big beating out beautiful right now?
Humble	A combination of gratitude with being honored and in recognition of mercy
Hungry	Starved, hangry (when hungry to the point of annoyance), and with voracious appetite
Hunted	Preyed upon, trapped, lured
Hurried	Bustled, hustled, and rushed
Hurt	Disappointed (oh – that word is the worst!), broken, damaged
Ideal	Right, perfect, as it (or one) should be and was meant to be
Ill	Sick, nauseous, woozy, or get specific: headache, stomach ache, feverish, etc.
Illecebrous	Chock one up for the gorgeous category! In this case, alluring, teasing, and flirtatious
Illogical	Unrealistic, ill-conceived, and unlikely
Immature	Childish (not child-like), irresponsible, and unaccountable
Impatient	Anxious, eager, restless, and edgy
Imperfect	Everybody ever except for Jesus and, of course, your newborn when you hold him or her, completely without fault
Imperious	Tyrannical, dictatorial, and full of harsh arrogance
Impious	Unfaithful, unbelieving, atheistic or agnostic
Impish	Spritely, playful, and devilish
Important	Valued and highly regarded
Impressed	Blown away, unexpectedly (and pleasantly) surprised, awed
Impressive	To be the subject of blowing away, pleasantly surprising, and awing others
Impulsive	Reactionary, impatient, daring
Incredible	Fabulous, amazing, and impressive to an unbelievable level
Indecisive	Wishy-washy, apprehensive, and weak-minded
Inflated	Arrogant, fake, self-important
Influential	Leaderly, guiding, and directing
Infuriated	Boiling over, raging, and hot-headed
Inquisitive	Why? Why do you want to know what that means? Why?
Insane	Crazy, mad, whirly-bird, coo-coo, and all of us a lot more than we'd like to admit

Insecure	Unsure, lacking in confidence
Insignificant	Unimportant, small, worthless (again – you're not)
Insistent	Encouraging, demanding (a positive, negative, and neutral take on the same sentiment . . . you'll enjoy our verbal emojis categories to come)
Insomniatic	Sleepless, alert, dazed
Inspired	Motivated, driven
Inspiring	To be the subject of motivating and driving others
Instinctive	Trusting of your feelings, like when a guy just seems a bit creepy – that feeling? Go with it
Intelligent	Smart, witty, well-read, educated, and mentally engaged
Interested	Piqued, curious
Interesting	When opening a gift you don't like: "That's...*interesting*." When learning about a field of study: "That's interesting." When discovering exciting knowledge: "How interesting!"
Interrupted	Knock Knock. **Who's there?** An interrupting cow. **An interrupting co—**MOO!
Intrigued	Interested, fascinated, captivated
Intriguing	To be the subject of interesting, fascinating, or captivating others
Introverted	Shy, closed, wall-flower
Intuitive	Mindful, reliant on instincts, inward-processing
Inundated	Overwhelmed, ganged up on, and attacked
Irksome	Bothersome, irritated, and annoyed
Irrational	Illogical, unrealistic, idealistic, mad, crazy, or unlikely
Irreplaceable	Unmatched, unique, and purposeful
Irritable	Annoyed, short-fused, and cold
Itchy	Scratchy
Jittery	Shaky, nervous and unsteady
Jolly	Happy, jovial, bouncy
Jovial	Happy, jolly, bouncy (ha!)
Joyful	Literally full of joy, deep internal happiness, grateful
Joyous	When the joy inside bursts out, glowing, exuberant
Judicious	Logical, thoughtful, objective, considerate (of facts)
Keen	Wise, thoughtful, and aware
Kept	Made safe (positive), held down as property (negative), and kept could be neutral
Kind	Sincere, nice, likeable, generous
Kindhearted	Genuinely loving
Lackadaisical	Uncaring, nonchalant, and unengaged
Lacking	Left wanting and falling short
Lamenting	Wailing, sobbing, and pessimistically focusing
Late	Tardy, behind
Laudable	Honorable, praise-worthy, respectable, and valued
Lazy	Lackadaisical, rested, and sloth-like

Lethargic	Dragging and slow, like a record player at the wrong speed; I know – more than half of the readers of this don't know what that sounds like
Lewd	Slimy, inappropriate, filthy, disrespectful, and even pornographic
Lively	Active, energetic, and alert
Livid	Angry, infuriated, and raging
Logical	Likely, realistic, and sensical
Longing	Yearning, desiring, and coveting
Loquacious	Chatty (positive), gossipy (negative), babbling (neutral); loose lips sink ships (negative), fluent in multiple languages (positive), he stammered on (neutral) . . . had to take some time with that one to get a little more . . . well, WORDY
Lost	Wandering, purposeless, directionless
Loved	Admired, adored, cherished, held
Lovely	What's the score of fat to fabulous, now?
Loving	Comforting, gentle, compassionate, and generous
Lucky	Blessed (which really isn't luck at all), prosperous
Magical	Whimsical, bewitching, spellbound
Majestic	Of great grandeur, amazement, and beauty to behold
Marginalized	Made insignificant, ignored, belittled
Marked	For what one is marked would completely change the meaning. Marked for promotion? Awesome! Marked for death . . . not so much
Marvelous	Dahling, you look mahvelous; it's wonderful – it's marvelous – it's delovely
Massive	Huge, enormous, gigantic, intrusive
Matchless	Irreplaceable, unbeatable
Mature	Responsible, accountable, grown-up
Mediocre	Average, mean, less than ideal
Meditative	Prayerful, peaceful, calm
Meek	Weak, small, and unimportant
Mellow	Still, problems lil', worries nil, and totally chill
Memorable	Remarkable, spotlighted
Mesmerizing	Engaging, astounding, and enchanting
Messy	Sloppy, dirty, unorganized, discombobulated
Methodical	Logical, process-driven, and organized
Mind-blowing	Positively remarkable and negatively unbelievable
Mindful	Pointed, self-aware, and plugged in
Miraculous	Unbelievable, faith-guided, wondrous
Mischievous	Sneaky, devilish, playfully disruptive; manage your mischief on the marauder's map
Miserable	Upset, depressed, down, and in need of company
Misguided	Misled, misdirected, led astray
Misjudged	Presumed something you are not

Misunderstood	Unheard, unrelated to, and not empathized or sympathized with
Modest	Covered up, careful, proper, prim, and protected
Monstrous	Raging, frothing, and vehemently angry or unloved
Moody	Hormonal and wishy-washy
Morose	Downtrodden, dark, gloomy, and death-focused
Motivated	Inspired, driven, guided
Mysterious	Unknown, incognito, sneaky
Naïve	Innocent and youthful
Natural	Not Lucille Ball's hair, Madonna's accent, or Dolly Parton's anything . . . what's *natural* is the timeless *nature* of the cultural pursuit of perfection
Naughty	Misbehaving, mischievous, and devilish
Nauseous	Sick, ill, vomiting, and green
Needed	Wanted, desired, purposeful
Needy	Dependent, clingy, and possibly bordering on burdensome
Neglected	Left behind, ignored, and mistreated
Nervous	Jittery, uncertain, worrisome
Notable	Remarkable, mentionable
Noticed	Observed, made aware, acknowledged
Oblivious	Unaware, ignorant, and blind to something or someone
Obtuse	Thick and ridiculously stupid
Odd	Unique, quirky, and eccentric
OK	A cousin to "fine"
Old	Antiquated and left behind or out-of-date
Open	Extraverted, willing, adventurous, and outgoing
Ordinary	Plain, simple, and unexciting
Organized	Methodical, logical, structured, process-driven
Orgasmic	The hopeful result of "Amatory" with your spouse
Outgoing	Open, extraverted, willing, and adventurous (ha!)
Outspoken	Blunt, brutally truthful, honest, our loud-mouthed (and a range of positive to negative implications)
Outstanding	Positively unique and incredible or negatively stood apart or freakish
Overawed	Alarmed, appalled, and flabbergasted, despite the "awed" portion of the word, sort of like INfamous does not mean "IN" famous; something the *Three Amigos* learned the hard way
Overcome	Beat, triumphed over, succeeded in
Overextended	Overtaxed, overworked, and overdid . . . usually to over-exhaustion
Overwhelmed	Negatively busy or swamped, but positively awed, such as being overwhelmed with gratitude or by the mercy of God
Parched	Dry and thirsty
Particular	Specific, picky, and judgmental
Passionate	Hot, feverish, and driven toward a particular goal
Pathetic	Pitiful, unworthy, and lowly

Patient	Calm and still
Peaceful	Calm and still accompanied by contentment and self-assuredness
Peachy	"Fine!" and "Outstanding!" (in word, but usually with great sarcasm)
Peppy	Jumpy, bouncy, happy, jubilant, and full of life
Perceptive	Observant, aware, and insightful
Perfect	Ideal, without fault and the first healthy cry of a newborn
Perplexed	Confused, confounded, and puzzled
Persevering	Determined, diligent, and driven
Persistent	Driven (possibly to annoyance), but toward a goal or vision
Phenomenal	UNBELIEVABLE (in the positive), that kid is a PHENOM! Amazing, talented, and awe-inspiring
Picky	Particular, fussy, and hard-to-please
Pious	Righteous
Playful	Youthful and joyous or not-so-youthful and mischievous
Pleased	Contented, satisfied, and fulfilled
Plucky	Bold, spritely, and spirited
Poised	Prim, proper, and put-together . . . perfectly
Poor	Broke, bankrupt, emptied
Positive	Optimistic, happy, and forward-looking
Powerful	Almighty, unbeatable, and grand
Practical	Realistic, logical, and left-brained
Praiseworthy	Laudable, honorable, respectable, admirable
Prayerful	Faithful, God-guided, and surrendered
Precious	Loved, held, kept, cherished, and honored
Predictable	Expected, anticipated, and likely
Preoccupied	Worried, concerned, nervous
Prepared	What all Boy Scouts should be!
Primed	Prepared, trained, educated, and made ready
Privileged	Oy! Do we want to get into this one, in today's politically charged climate? We all are and none of us are for various reasons. We are privileged with what we have been given in opportunities and relationships. We are not for what we have been given in obstacles and hardships.
Prized	Valued and treasured
Protected	Safe and cared for
Protective	Hovering and mothering
Proud	Boastful, accomplished, triumphant, confident
Puffy	D'oh! Another one for the huge column!
Purposeful	Guided, directed, uniquely skilled
Pushy	Bossy
Puzzled	Confounded, confused, and perplexed
Puzzling	To be the subject of confounding, confusing, and perplexing others

Queasy	Nauseous, often for non-physical or physiological reasons, sick, ill, woozy, or disgusted
Querulous	Inquisitive, questioning, curious
Questioning	Inquisitive, querulous, curious (ha!)
Quick	Fast, efficient, simple
Quiet	Peaceful, calm, still
Racy	Teasing, sexy, alluring, scandalous
Randy	Horny, playful, dirty
Rare	Unique, individual, distinctive
Rational	Logical, realistic, pragmatic
Ravenous	Hungry, desirous, voracious
Ready	Trained, educated, prepared, at the help
Receptive	Open-minded, flexible, brainstorming
Recognizable	Noticeable, acknowledged, seen
Refreshed	Awake, alert, revived, rejuvenated
Regretful	Guilty, ashamed, sorrowful, sorry, apologetic
Rejuvenated	Awake, alert, revived, refreshed (ha!)
Relaxed	Laid back, calm, carefree
Reliable	Responsible, accountable, trustworthy
Relieved	The feeling after a rest stop following a long car ride and three cups of coffee . . . ahhh. Also achievable through the settling of mind and heart
Relished	To fully take in a moment or achievement of yourself or another; positively "I relished the opportunity to lead the organization to victory." Negatively "She relished the fact that her husband's sleazy ex had gained 150 pounds."
Remarkable	Noticeable, observed, noted, amazing, impressive, sighted with grandeur
Renewed	Brought back to life, rejuvenated, revived
Resigned	Accepting, compliant, and subdued
Resolute	Decided, set
Respected	Valued, honored, treasured, and admired
Responsive	Engaged, reactive, alert, involved
Rested	Refreshed, calm
Restful	Lazing, laid back, at peace
Revived	Awake, alert, refreshed, revived (déjà vu)
Rewarded	Treated, prized, awarded, recognized
Rich	Prosperous, blessed, lucky
Risky	Endangered, dicey, unsafe, not recommended, reckless
Riveted	Engaged, on-the-edge-of-your-seat, as a rivet attaches things together, a person becomes attached to an activity or observation
Riveting	To be the subject of attachment
Rude	Mean, nasty, uncaring, thoughtless, snobbishness
Ruffled	Flustered, thrown off, and shaken (*and* stirred)

Rushed	Hustled, bustled, quickened, scurried
Sacred	Glorified, honored, blessed
Sad	Down, blue, depressed, melancholy, upset
Safe	Cautionary, prudent, reserved
Sagacious	Perceptive, witty, ingenious
Sane	Mindful, logical, together
Sarcastic	In the words of Morgan Freeman, "The ability to insult stupid people without them realizing it." In many relationships, a love language
Sassy	Smart-mouthed, wise-assed
Satisfied	Content and accomplished, but perhaps with an air of minimalism
Scared	Frightened, fearful, afraid, worrisome
Scarred	Broken, damaged, jaded, once-bitten
Scrawny	Little, tiny, insignificant, weak
Secure	Safe, protected, unshakable
Seeking	Searching, lost, guided
Seen	Spotted, recognized, acknowledged
Selfish	Egotistical, self-serving, and thoughtless toward others
Selfless	Generous, giving, and outward-looking
Sensational	Marvelous, remarkable, unbelievable (positively)
Sensible	Logical, realistic, methodical, and pragmatic
Sensitive	Emotional, dramatic, feeling
Sensual	Sexy, attractive (BOOM!), alluring
Set	Fixed, resolute, unbending, assured
Sexy	Attractive (BOOM, AGAIN!), teasing, beautiful, hot
Shaky	Flustered, jittery
Sharp	Smart, intelligent, witty, wise
Sheltered	Protected, naïve, innocent
Shining	Glowing, exuberant, jubilant, effervescent
Shiny	Sparkling, glamorous, glowing
Short-tempered	Short-fused, annoyed, irritable, moody
Shrewd	Keen and slick
Shy	Timid, bashful, introverted
Sick	Ill, nauseous, woozy, queasy, dizzy, faint, disgusted
Significant	Important, valued, treasured, cherished, loved
Silent	Quiet, left out, unheard
Simple	Easy, quick, efficient, and "Elementary, my dear Watson."
Sleepy	Tired, drowsy, drained, sluggish
Sluggish	Tired, drowsy, drained, and sleepy (ha!)
Small	Little, tiny, insignificant, unimportant
Smart	Witty, intelligent, wise, keen, street-smart, educated, well-read
Smiley	Happy, glowing, basking
Smooth	Suave, flirtatious, masterful
Smug	Full of arrogant intellect, know-it-all, pompous

Snug	Cuddly, cozy, warm, safe
Sophisticated	Prim, proper, professional, put together
Sore	Achy, hurting, raw
Sorrowful	Apologetic, guilty, remorseful
Sought	Chased, desired, wooed
Special	Positively unique, negatively different and left out
Speechless	……
Spent	Drained, exhausted
Spicy	Hot, alluring, sexy, suave
Spirited	Spritely, plucky, bodacious, and bold
Splendid	Joyous and delighted
Spontaneous	Impulsive, daring, unscheduled
Stable	Strong, reliable, accountable, responsible, mature
Stagnant	Still, unmoving, stale, plateauing
Starving	Hungry, emaciated, voracious
Static	Unchanging with negative connotation
Stationary	Unmoving (by the way, the paper is spelled "stationEry")
Steadfast	Unchanging with positive connotation, guaranteed, reliable, and accountable
Stiff	Unbending and inflexible; "He has such a stick up his butt!"
Still	Peaceful, calm, relaxed, and content
Stimulated	Alert, turned on, energized
Stinky	Rotten, repugnant, malodorous
Stirred	Moved to emotion and, often, to action
Strained	Stretched, over-exerted
Strange	Weird, odd, eccentric, eclectic
Stressed	Overwhelmed, panicky, wrought
Stretched	Developed, grown, flexed
Striving	Driving, motivating, persisting
Strong	Courageous, healthy, bold, built
Strong-minded	Stubborn, prideful
Stubborn	Prideful, strong-minded
Stuck	Directionless, lost, left behind, unchanging, and unmoving
Stuffed	Full, bloated, well-fed
Stunning	See "attractive"
Stylish	Trendy, fashionable, chic
Suggestive	Alluring, teasing, sexy, sleazy
Sulky	Mopey, sad, upset, depressed, melancholy
Super	Upbeat, energized, revitalized, unbelievable, but sometimes said with a note of sarcasm
Superb	See "super", but less often used with sarcasm
Superior	Arrogant, set-apart, above others
Supported	Comforted, empathized with, backed up
Supportive	The source of another's comfort, empathy, and backing up
Surprised	Shocked, awed, disbelieving

Surprising	To be unexpected and unpredictable
Surrendered	Prayerful, submissive, given in or up
Suspicious	Untrusting, doubtful, cynical
Swamped	Overwhelmed, busy, buried
Sweet	Kind, nice, liked, adorable
Swollen	And we were on a roll…another fat, big, engorged, huge, bulging, abnormal type of word
Sympathetic	Compassion for another's feelings (empathy differs as it is showing compassion for another's feelings to which you can specifically relate)
Taciturn	Intentionally cold, distant, and aloof
Targeted	Marked, cornered, hunted, preyed upon, attacked
Taxed	Overworked, exhausted, spent
Temperamental	Moody, hormonal, short-fused
Tenacious	Diligent, hard-working
Tender	Sweet, compassionate, gentle, kind
Tense	Stressed, tight, wrought
Terrific	Today, awesome and wonderful; in original English, terrifying and horrible
Thankful	Grateful, appreciative, humbled, blessed
Thirsty	Parched, dry, dehydrated
Thoughtful	Outward-looking, generous, kind
Thrilled	Excited, exuberant, joyful
Tight	Stiff, penny-pinching
Timely	Prompt, idyllic, coincidental
Timid	Shy, bashful, reserved, introverted, quiet
Tired	Sleepy
Toasted	Drunk, trashed, loaded, hosed, gooned, effed, three sheets to the wind
Toasty	Warm, cozy, snug, cuddly
Touching	Moving (emotionally), inspiring
Tranquil	Peaceful, calm, still, restful
Transfixed	Focused, obsessed, drilled on
Transformed	Changed, evolved
Transforming	Transitioning, changing, growing
Transparent	Honest, truthful, open-book
Traumatized	Emotionally destroyed, wrecked, stunned beyond normal function
Treasured	Cherished, valued, honored
Tremendous	Grand, magnificent, amazing
Trendy	Chic, fashionable, stylish, popular
Troubled	Worried, upset, disappointed, hurt
Trusted	To be thought reliable, dependable, and accountable
Trustful	To easily assign traits of reliability, dependability, and accountability to others

Trusting	To allow others to earn the titles of reliable, dependable, and accountable
Trustworthy	To *actually* be reliable, dependable, and accountable based on a record of those traits
Turgid	Bloated and distended
Unbelievable	Usually not actually without belief, but an expression of amazement, whether negative or positive. "How was your day at work?" "UNBELIEVABLE!"
Uncertain	Unknowing, unsure
Unchanging	Unmoving, fixed, stagnant, static
Uncomfortable	Fidgety, cramped, awkward
Understood	Known, presumed
Undervalued	Underappreciated
Undisturbed	Left alone, not bothered
Uneasy	Queasy, upset, nauseous (sometimes for emotional reasons rather than physiological)
Unfocused	Unengaged, distracted
Unhappy	Sad, discontented, unsatisfied, disappointed
Unimportant	Insignificant, small, meaningless
Unique	Individual, special, distinctive
Unpredictable	Spontaneous, erratic, whimsical, wayward
Unprepared	NOT a Boy Scout!
Unrecognizable	Greatly changed, unknown, mistaken
Unrelenting	Persistent, pursuant, driven
Unruffled	Strong, unshaken, orderly
Unsettled	Worried, concerned, uneasy
Unshakable	Resolved, resolute, unbending, assured
Unstable	Mad, crazy, insane, unpredictable, changing
Unsteady	Imbalanced, jittery, shaky
Unsure	Uncertain, unknown, timid, pensive, contemplative
Untiring	Eager, relentless, persistent
Unwanted	Undesired, unloved, plain, forgotten
Unwearied	Tireless, incessant, indefatigable
Upset	Hurt, disappointed, sad, or emotionally ill
Used	Abused, taken advantage of, exploited
Useful	Purposeful, guided, important, significant
Valiant	Like the Prince, but braver than he is charming
Valuable	Treasured, cherished, honored
Vehement	Emphatic force, often added to negative statements: "I vehemently disagree," or "I vehemently refuse to go with that man on the trip because I hate him."
Victorious	Triumphant, proud, accomplished
Vigilant	Watchfully observant
Virtuous	Keeping one's values and morals in tact
Vital	Necessary, important

Vivacious	Lively, effervescent, full of joy, exuberant
Volatile	Violent, explosive, hot-headed
Voracious	Starved (not necessarily for food), ravenous
Vulnerable	Exposed, open, honest, on display
Wanted	Lusty, desired, sexy, or – non-relationally, pursued, chased, and wooed
Wanting	Desirous, covetous
Warm	Cozy, snug, comfortable
Watchful	Observant, suspicious
Weak	Frail, delicate, small, meek
Weary	Tired, worn out, run down
Wise	Smart, intelligent, street-smart, knowing
Wistful	Dreamy, forlorn, yearning
Withdrawn	Reserved, wall-flower, shy, distant
Withered	Frail, weakened, ill, shrunken
Woeful	Piteous, tragic, mournful
Wonderful	Glorious, stupendous, amazing
Woozy	Queasy, dizzy, uneasy, nauseous, light-headed, faint
Wordy	This list . . . but we've only just begun! Wait until you get to the whole part on "how you use them in your writing"! You will be an expert Experimental Word Player by the end of the book!
Worldly	Knowledgeable, usually through experience, but sometimes through education, of places beyond your current location of residence
Worn	Exhausted, surrendered, submissive, defeated, deflated, beaten
Worried	Troubled, concerned, preoccupied . . . try the serenity prayer: "God, grant me the serenity to accept the things I cannot change, the courage to change the things I can, and the wisdom to know the difference." (Then check out the verbal emojis for courageous and wise!)
Worthwhile	Of value
Worthy	You are infinitely worthy and unconditionally loved. VALUED, TREASURED, CHERISHED, ADORED, PURPOSEFUL, RESPECTED, HONORED, PROTECED, BRILLIANT, BELIEVED, CALLED, AFFIRMED, SAVED, COVERED, KEPT, HELD, MAINTAINED, PLEASING, CHOSEN, GOOD, ACCEPTED, UPRIGHT, LAUDABLE, RIGHTEOUS, PRAISEWORTHY, PRICELESS, PURE, AND EXCELLENT
Wounded	Hurt, offended, broken, damaged, injured
Wowed	Amazed, blown away
Wretched	Wicked, evil, devilish
Yearning	Longing, wistful, desirous, covetous
Young	Naïve, innocent, child-like, beautiful
Zealous	Eager . . . to dive into the word play in the pages ahead!

Word

Word Play!

Play

Word Play!

Word

Play

Play

Word

WORD PLAY!

WORD PLAY . . . YOUR Verbal Emojis Dictionary and Thesaurus

I bet you're wishing you weren't such an overachiever in creating all of those extra verbal emojis, now!

This is the part of the book when you create your own definitions and synonyms for your own verbal emojis list. Don't be ridiculous about it.

"Happy" is not "Sad," for instance. You should still start out with those great, tried-and-true, time-tested dictionaries and thesauruses. Then, add your own flair and understanding to your verbal emojis definitions and synonyms.

Use the boxes below and on the next few pages to define and find synonyms for some or all of the verbal emojis you wrote down in your first word play. If you prefer, you could also add to the definitions and synonyms created in the list of 700+ Verbal Emojis or come up with even MORE words and phrases of your own to put meanings or synonyms to in the table, below.

WORD OR PHRASE	DEFINITION AND SYNONYMS

WORD OR PHRASE	DEFINITION AND SYNONYMS

WORD OR PHRASE	DEFINITION AND SYNONYMS

WORD OR PHRASE	DEFINITION AND SYNONYMS

WORD OR PHRASE	DEFINITION AND SYNONYMS

WORD OR PHRASE	DEFINITION AND SYNONYMS

Upside-Downed

UPSIDE-DOWNED

VERBAL

Emojis

Upside-Downed

Verbal

Emojis

Emojis

Verbal

44

Upside-Downed Verbal Emojis

What would a list of verbal emojis be without providing suitable antonyms? Of course, in our definitions, we shared an average of three synonyms. As for the antonyms, let's do as Grandma used to say and, "turn that frown upside down!"

Let's upside down some of those emojis to find their contrasts, their opposites, the negated definitions. Wait a minute — those are all synonyms . . . but FOR antonyms. Try to find a set of emojis for that paragraph!

The point of this book is to help you, as readers, find the right words to express your characters' emotions, right? Well, that's one of the points. We also have to help you, as writers, express your characters' emotions while retaining the essence of your character.

*Let's say your character is not a **patient** person. You may think, 'No problem. I'll look up synonyms and definitions for **impatient** and see if that works.' But, when you see that "not accepting delay, and anxious" still don't work, how about trying the antonyms of patient? Troubled . . . frustrated . . . AGITATED! Yes, that is how your character feels! (By the way, consider that bonus #705!)*

Antonyms of your character's opposite emotion may sometimes be more accurate than synonyms of your character's actual feeling . . . er . . . verbal emoji. Say that three times fast!

*Well, you get the idea. Basically, we've provided a whole lot of words, but we've got even more to give to you so that you'll be able to make your characters as expressive (nay, more!) than your average yellow-faced digital character set. So without further ado, I present to you, the upside-downed verbal emojis according to an **Experimental Word Player**. Shagadelic, baby.*

WORD OR PHRASE	~~ANTONYMS~~ UPSIDE-DOWNED VERBAL EMOJIS
Abnormous	Normally-sized, average
Absent	Present, engaged, included
Absorbed	Distracted, unfocused, lost
Absorbing	Excluding, ignoring, oblivious
Absurd	Normal, practical, predictable
Achy	Healthy, active, strong
Active	Lazy, lackadaisical, relaxed
Admired	Disrespected, unknown, ignored, disliked, criticized, detested
Adorable	Ugly, unattractive: "Oh! It's a . . . *baby*."
Adored	Unloved, forgotten, unremarkable
Adrift	Focused, driven, motivated
Adroit	Ignorant, dense, unintelligent
Adventurous	Timid, reclusive, safe
Affectionate	Cold, aloof, distant
Affirmed	Denied, disproven
Affluent	Poor, weak, forgotten, forsaken
Aggressive	Gentle, calm, kind
Agitated	Peaceful, agreeable, composed
Agreeable	Irritable, defiant, bossy
Ahead	Behind, lacking, failing
Alert	Drifting, drowsy, inattentive
Alive	Dying, weak, frail,
Alluring	Turnoff, disgusting, revolting
Altruistic	Greedy, stingy, cheap
Amatory	Clumsy, unattractive, entrapping
Amazed	Blasé, bored, uninspired
Amazing	Boring, uninspiring
Ambitious	Lazy, uninterested, nonchalant
Angry	Calm, agreeable, happy
Animated	Stiff, dry, cold
Annoyed	Happy, inspired, bubbly
Anticipatory	Dreading, pessimistic
Antiquated	Youthful, innocent, naïve, new, fresh, green
Antsy	Still, peaceful, calm
Anxious	Unworried, surrendered, accepting
Apathetic	Driven, passionate, fervent
Appreciated	Forgotten, ignored, taken for granted
Appreciative	Ungrateful, thankless
Apprehensive	Spontaneous, impulsive
Aroused	Uninterested, turned off
Articulate	Slurring, drawling, babbling, incomprehensible
Artistic	Uncreative, unimaginative, left-brained
Ashamed	Proud, boastful, glad

Assiduous	Lazy, lethargic, uninvolved
Astonishing	Normal, ordinary, unimpressive
Astounded	Unimpressed
Astounding	Boring, everyday, blasé
Attentive	Oblivious, ignorant, uninterested
Attractive	Ugly, uninteresting
Audacious	Uncaring, apathetic
Avid	Weak, untrained, unskilled
Awake	Asleep
Awakened	Put to sleep
Aware	Unaware, oblivious
Awed	Bored, predictable
Awe-inspiring	Uninspiring, blasé faire
Awesome	Plain, expected
Awkward	Sophisticated, elegant, graceful
Bashful	Bold, extraverted, daring, outspoken
Beaten	Triumphant, raging, driven
Beautiful	Haggard, homely, frumpy
Behind	Ahead, advanced
Beloved	Hated, despised, disliked
Besieged	Let go, released
Bewitching	Uncaptivating, plain, uninteresting
Big	Small, tiny, miniscule, unimportant
Bitter	Innocent, awed, fresh
Blasé	Exciting, new, interesting
Blessed	Forsaken, forgotten
Blissful	Miserable, depressed, blue
Bloated	Slender, svelte
Blue	Happy, up, exuberant
Bogglish	Ahead, wise
Bold	Shy, quiet, timid
Bored	Excited, engaged, absorbed
Boring	Thrilling, joyous
Bossy	Timid, submissive
Bouncy	Dragging, weary
Brainy	Dull, unintelligent, stupid, dumb, behind
Brave	Cowardly, apathetic
Breathtaking	Plain, ordinary, simple
Bright	Dull, dark, foggy
Brilliant	Unintelligent, stupid, dull
Bubbly	Miserable, lethargic
Bulging	Skinny, slender, thin, fit, shapely
Busy	Bored, calm, under control
Calm	Panicked, flustered, hurried, hustled, bustled

Candid	Dishonest, diplomatic, sarcastic
Capable	Unable, untrained, uneducated, unwilling
Carefree	Burdened, responsible, accountable
Caring	Uncaring or careless, thoughtless
Casual	Formal, professional, sophisticated
Certain	Unsure, apprehensive
Changing	Stagnant, static, still, unmoving
Charmed	Turned off, unimpressed
Charming	Disconnecting, alarming
Chaste	Sleazy, slutty, loose
Cheerful	Downer, negative, unhappy
Cheery	Blue, sad, melancholy
Cherished	Neglected, ignored, unloved
Chic	Out-of-style, unfashionable
Childish	Mature, stately, worldly, sophisticated
Claustrophobic	Open, crowd-loving, close-talker
Clean	Dirty, filthy, disorganized, wreck
Clever	Slow, dull, unwitting
Clingy	Distant, disconnected
Closed	Open, extraverted, bold, vulnerable
Cold	Warm, comforting, gentle, compassionate, sympathetic,
Collected	Frantic, panicked, disorganized
Colossal	Small, unimportant, normal
Comely	Homely, ugly
Comfortable	Awkward, cramped
Comforting	Uncaring
Commendable	Unimportant, negligible, disregarding
Compassionate	Cold, uncaring, thoughtless
Complex	Easy, simple
Complicated	Easy, simple
Composed	Falling apart, broken down, wreck
Concerned	Apathetic, unworried, relaxed
Confident	Insecure, bashful, uncertain
Confused	Assured, positive
Constrained	Unrestrained, loose, outspoken
Consumed	Forgetful, unengaged, uninterested
Contemplative	Thoughtless, impulsive, spontaneous
Content	Unhappy, dissatisfied, joyless
Cool	Warm, loving, gentle
Courageous	Fearful, insecure, timid
Coveted	Thrown away, tossed, unwanted
Cowardly	Courageous, heroic, brave
Cozy	Uncomfortable, awkward, uneasy
Crafty	Dull, unimaginative, uncreative

Creative	Drab, left-brained
Creepy	Comfortable, at ease, relaxed
Crushed	Lifted up, exalted, exuberant, effervescent
Curvaceous	Stick-like, slender
Cynical	Faithful, believing
Damaged	Unbroken, innocent
Daring	Timid, afraid, scrupulous
Dazzling	Plain, simple, uninteresting
Decisive	Wishy-washy, apprehensive, contemplative
Dehydrated	Full, well-hydrated
Dejected	Appreciated, joyful
Delayed	On time, prompt, timely
Delicate	Tough, resilient, strong, unbreakable
Delighted	Saddened, disappointed
Dependable	Immature, unreliable
Depleted	Replenished, revived, refreshed, rejuvenated
Depressed	Happy, upbeat, manic
Desired	Unwanted, left behind, neglected
Desolate	Crowded, surrounded
Determined	Apathetic, uninterested, lazy
Difficult	Easy, simplistic
Diplomatic	Blunt, candid, cruel
Disbelieving	Faithful, prayerful, believing
Dissatisfied	Contented, happy, satisfied
Distended	Hungry, voracious, plenty of room
Distinctive	Repeatable, average, normal
Distracted	Consumed, engaged, focused, absorbed
Distressed	Calm, relaxed, peaceful
Distrustful	Trusting, believing, vulnerable
Disturbed	At ease
Dizzy	Strong, stable, confident
Docile	Active, busy, diligent
Doubtful	Believing, faithful, surrendered
Dowdy	Beautiful, stunning, attractive
Down	Up, happy, blissful
Drained	Bubbly, giddy, exuberant
Dramatic	Unresponsive, emotionless
Dreaming	Logical, realistic
Dreamy	Pragmatic, methodical
Driving	Lazing, quitting
Drowsy	Sleepy, dragging, tired
Dry	Wet, hydrated
Dubious	Believing, faithful, miraculous
Dull	Sharp, witty, smart

Eager	Uninterested, lazy
Earnest	Dispassionate, frigid, indifferent
Easygoing	Stressed, manic, frantic, panicked
Ebullient	Dull, unattached
Ecstatic	Dejected
Edgy	Following norms, sticking to the status quo
Effervescent	Deflated, down, beaten
Egocentric	Generous, selfless, giving
Egotistic	Philanthropic, altruistic
Embarrassed	Proud, triumphant, boastful
Emotional	Straight-faced, dull, inexpressive
Empowered	Weakened, emasculated
Empty	Full, spirited
Encouraged	Discouraged, let down, beaten
Encouraging	Talking down, belittling
Energized	Weakened, depressed
Engaged	Uninterested, apathetic, ignorant
Engorged	Small, shrinking
Engrossed	Ignorant
Enjoyable	A turn off, unimpressed
Enlivened	Weakened, unininteresting
Enraged	Calming, tranquilizing
Enthralling	Deflating, disengaging
Enthusiastic	Bored
Enticing	Not tempting, passable
Equipped	Unready, unprepared
Erotic	Plain, puritan
Erratic	Expected
Esteemed	Disrespected, unworthy
Estimable	Dishonorable, poor
Estranged	Close, connected
Evolving	Unchanging
Exalted	Put down, belittled
Excellent	Weak, common, crude
Exceptional	Plain, ordinary
Excited	Uninterested, blasé
Exhausted	Alert, awake, refreshed
Expanded	Shrunken
Expanding	Shrinking
Expectant	Procrastinating, putting off, dreading
Experienced	Unskilled, untrained, unprepared
Explosive	Calm, still, stagnant
Exposed	Cold, stiff, stubborn
Expressive	Straight-faced, unemotional

Exquisite	Simple
Extraordinary	Ordinary, common, plain
Extroverted	Introverted, shy, bashful, timid
Exultant	Submissive, repressive
Fabulous	Plain, uninteresting
Faint	Strong, lively
Fake	Genuine, sincere
Famous	Unknown, discreet
Fantastic	Unimpressive
Fascinated	Bored, unimpressed
Fascinating	Common, ordinary
Fashionable	Out-of-style, out-of-date
Fat	Thin, slender, skinny
Fatigued	Alert, awake, lively
Favored	Forgotten, forsaken
Fearful	Bold, daring, adventurous
Fearless	Courageous, careless
Feeble	Strong, able-bodied
Fervent	Dispassionate, apathetic
Fiery	Dull, disengaged, uncaring
Fine	Fine
Firm	Flexible, bending, changeable
Flabbergasted	Unsurprising, Expecting
Flattered	Uninterested, turned off
Floppy	Stiff, tight, unbending
Flummoxed	Predicted
Flushed	Pale
Focused	Disengaged, oblivious
Foggy	Focused, alert
Foreign	Common, relatable
Forgetful	Memorable
Forlorn	Letting go, releasing, not missing
Fortunate	Unlucky, cursed
Fragile	Strong, stable
Frail	Unbreakable, mended
Frantic	Calm, stable
Fraught	Peaceful, at ease
Frazzled	Relaxed, stable, calm
Free	Tied down, accountable
Fresh	Wilted, weathered
Friendly	Cold, stand-offish, distant
Frightened	Brave, courageous, plucky, bold
Frisky	Cold, not playful, stiff
Fulfilled	Empty

Full	Barren
Functional	Broken, damaged, unskilled
Funny	Serious, common
Generous	Stingy, greedy, penny-pinching
Gentle	Calm, comforting
Gigantic	Small, tiny, miniscule
Glad	Unhappy, downtrodden
Gloomy	Upbeat, optimistic
Glum	Joyful
Gorgeous	Ugly, unattractive
Grand	Discreet, unnoticeable
Grateful	Unappreciative, thankless
Gratified	Dissatisfied, unproven
Great	Unwell
Greedy	Philanthropic, altruistic, selfless
Groggy	Alert, engaged, lively
Growing	Shrinking, reducing
Guilty	Innocent, proud
Gutsy	Timid, shaky, unsure
Hairy	Bare, nude, smooth
Happy	Discontented, unhappy
Hardened	Soft, innocent, fresh, green, naïve
Hard-working	Lazy, lethargic, apathetic
Harmless	Violent, harmful, dangerous
Hassled	Unbothered, available
Haunted	Free-spirited, cheerful
Heavy	Light-hearted, free
Heroic	Cowardly, yellow
Hesitant	Spontaneous, impromptu
Hidden	Conspicuous, obvious, in-your-face
Hilarious	Serious, sarcastic, dark
Hip	Unfashionable, out-of-style, out-of-date, not with the times
Hollow	Full, fulfilled, overflowing
Honest	Dishonest, untruthful, untrustworthy
Honored	Dishonored, disrespectful
Hopeful	Hopeless, despondent, in despair
Hormonal	Even-keeled, stable
Hot	Cold, dispassionate
Hubristic	Humble, modest
Huge	Small, tiny, bitty
Humble	Arrogant, prideful, egotistical
Hungry	Full, stuffed
Hunted	Threatening, empowering
Hurried	Slowed down, relaxed, paced

Hurt	Mended, healed, well
Ideal	Imperfect, incorrect, unfitting
Ill	Well, healthy, vibrant, vital
Illecebrous	Unattractive, repulsive
Illogical	Thoughtful, predictable, realistic
Immature	Responsible, dependable, accountable
Impatient	Patient, accommodating
Imperfect	Perfect, flawless, Christ
Imperious	Humble, submissive, obedient
Impious	Holy, faithful, righteous
Impish	Grand, larger-than-life, a good fairy
Important	Insignificant, meaningless
Impressed	Uninterested, bored
Impressive	Plain, common, ordinary
Impulsive	Planned, strategic, outlined
Incredible	Believable, every day, status quo, norm
Indecisive	Decisive, firm, confident
Inflated	Deflated, dejected, worn down
Influential	Disconnected, unfollowed
Infuriated	Calm, relaxed, agreeable
Inquisitive	Unquestioning
Insane	Sane, stable, calm
Insecure	Confident, proud, self-assured
Insignificant	Meaningful, impacting, purposeful
Insistent	Giving, submissive, surrendered
Insomniatic	Zzzzzz……….
Inspired	Unmotivated, bored
Inspiring	Uninteresting
Instinctive	Thought through, unnatural
Intelligent	Dull, stupid, dumb
Interested	Disregarding
Interesting	Not intriguing
Interrupted	Continuing, going on, flowing forward . . .
Intrigued	Disinterested
Intriguing	Boring
Introverted	Extraverted, bold, outgoing, outspoken
Intuitive	Logical, planned, strategic
Inundated	Left alone, ignored
Irksome	Inspiring, engaging
Irrational	Rational, realistic, pragmatic
Irreplaceable	Replaceable, normal
Irritable	Enjoyable
Itchy	Soothing
Jittery	Still, calm, stable

Jolly	Downtrodden, melancholy, blue
Jovial	Unhappy, heavy, burdened
Joyful	Sad, unfulfilled
Joyous	Empty
Judicious	Subjective
Keen	Dull
Kept	Freed, released
Kind	Cold, uncaring
Kindhearted	Thoughtless, blind to the world
Lackadaisical	Diligent, earnest, hard-working
Lacking	Prosperous
Lamenting	Praising
Late	On time, timely, prompt
Laudable	Illegitimate, unworthy, dishonorable
Lazy	Hard-working
Lethargic	Active, energetic, bubbly
Lewd	Chaste, righteous, pious
Lively	Lethargic, lazy
Livid	Joyful, exuberant
Logical	Illogical, unrealistic
Longing	Releasing, letting go, setting free
Loquacious	Subdued, restrained
Lost	Found, discovered
Loved	Hated, despised
Lovely	Repulsive
Loving	Cold, apathetic, hate-filled
Lucky	Unlucky, cursed
Magical	Normal, expected
Majestic	Plain, common, ordinary
Marginalized	Exalted, glorified
Marked	Ignored, overlooked
Marvelous	Simple, unimpressive
Massive	Small, tiny, miniscule, itty bitty
Matchless	Matched, marked, paired off
Mature	Immature, irresponsible
Mediocre	Above average, ahead, successful
Meditative	Frantic, panicked, worrisome
Meek	Bold, arrogant
Mellow	Manic, excitable
Memorable	Forgettable
Mesmerizing	Uninteresting, non-remarkable
Messy	Clean, organized, structured
Methodical	Unplanned, spontaneous
Mind-blowing	Ordinary, expected, average, normal

Mindful	Unaware, oblivious
Miraculous	Plain, normal
Mischievous	Rule-following, prudent
Miserable	Uplifted, happy, joyful
Misguided	Led, guided, purpose-driven
Misjudged	Categorized
Misunderstood	Understood, empathized with
Modest	Loose, sleazy, open
Monstrous	Human, kindly
Moody	Stable, unchanging, calm
Morose	Optimistic, upbeat
Motivated	Lethargic, stuck
Mysterious	Obvious, clear
Naïve	Aware, jaded
Natural	Plastic, fake
Naughty	Behaving, sinless
Nauseous	Well, healthy, vivacious
Needed	Unwanted, unnecessary
Needy	Independent
Neglected	Cared for, watched over, hovered
Nervous	Confident, calm, assured
Notable	Uninteresting, non-remarkable
Noticed	Missed, forgot, lost
Oblivious	Aware, observant
Obtuse	Wise, keen, sharp-witted
Odd	Normal, status quo, expected
OK	OK
Old	Young, innocent, new, fresh, green
Open	Closed, close-minded, distant, recluse
Ordinary	Extraordinary, amazing, incredible, fabulous
Organized	Disorganized, cluttered, messy
Orgasmic	Faking it
Outgoing	Quiet, reserved, timid
Outspoken	Restrained, constrained
Outstanding	Simple, wall-flower
Overawed	Soothing, calming
Overcome	Unimpressed
Overextended	Underworked
Overwhelmed	Skating by or through, unchallenged
Parched	Quenched, filled, satisfied
Particular	Not picky, agreeable
Passionate	Dispassionate, uninterested, apathetic
Pathetic	Admirable, honorable, respectable
Patient	Impatient, agitated

Peaceful	Frantic, manic, crazy, insane
Peachy	*Actually* peachy
Peppy	Dragging, lethargic, drowsy
Perceptive	Oblivious, blind, unnoticing
Perfect	Imperfect, flawed, unfitting
Perplexed	Easy, simple, figureable, puzzleable
Persevering	Quitting, giving up, giving in
Persistent	Submitting, accepting defeat
Phenomenal	Normal, status quo, average
Picky	Agreeable, easy-to-please
Pious	Self-righteous, arrogant
Playful	Strict, straight-laced
Pleased	Displeased, unsatisfied
Plucky	Timid, shy, bashful
Poised	Clumsy, clown-like, jesterly (and yes, I made that word up!)
Poor	Prosperous, wealthy, rich
Positive	Negative, neutral, pragmatic
Powerful	Weak, downtrodden, beaten
Practical	Dreamy, illogical, imaginative, head-in-the-clouds
Praiseworthy	Dishonorable, unrespectable
Prayerful	Disbelieving, unfaithful
Precious	Worthless, value-less
Predictable	Unplanned, unexpected, surprising
Preoccupied	Calm, relaxed, unworried
Prepared	Unskilled, unready
Primed	Untrained, uneducated, unprepared
Privileged	Disenfranchised
Prized	Forgotten, neglected, unimportant
Protected	Exposed, susceptible
Protective	Negligent
Proud	Ashamed, guilty, abashed
Puffy	Thin, svelte, fit
Purposeful	Aimless, drifting, wandering, lost
Pushy	Subdued, submissive, agreeable
Puzzled	Astounded
Puzzling	Figured, simplified
Queasy	Healthy, well, stable, strong
Querulous	Unquestioning
Questioning	Accepting
Quick	Slow, lethargic
Quiet	Loud, bold, outspoken
Racy	Quiet, modest, prim
Randy	Proper, clean, virtuous
Rare	Normal, unimportant, dime a dozen

Rational	Illogical, unrealistic
Ravenous	Full, unwanting
Ready	Unprepared
Receptive	Close-mined, unaccepting, stiff
Recognizable	Incognito, in disguise, hidden
Refreshed	Drained, emptied
Regretful	Unashamed, guiltless, unapologetic
Rejuvenated	Exhausted, spent, wasted
Relaxed	Stressed, distressed, manic, frantic
Reliable	Undependable, unaccountable
Relieved	Worried, concerned, panicked
Relished	Abhorred, condemned
Remarkable	Unnoticeable
Renewed	Done, finished
Resigned	Feisty, driving, aiming
Resolute	Unsure, indecisive
Respected	Dishonored, unloved, neglected
Responsive	Unconscious, unaware
Rested	Wiped out, run down
Restful	Agitated, fidgety
Revived	Graying, withered
Rewarded	Ignored, forgotten, overlooked
Rich	Poor, in need
Risky	Safe, secure, protected
Riveted	Bored, uninterested
Riveting	Disengaging
Rude	Kind, warm, understanding
Ruffled	Stable, calm, at peace
Rushed	Paced, at ease
Sacred	Impious, prideful
Sad	Happy, content, upbeat
Safe	Endangered, at risk, perilous
Sagacious	Foolish, idiotic, imbecile
Sane	Crazy, mad
Sarcastic	Sincere, genuine, kind
Sassy	Sweet, endearing, dainty
Satisfied	Discontented, hungry, thirsty, desirous
Scared	Brave, heroic
Scarred	Healed, well, mended
Scrawny	Brawny, large, strong
Secure	Unconfident, unsure
Seeking	Secure, found
Seen	Incognito, hidden, obscured
Selfish	Selfless, giving, generous

Selfless	Arrogant, egocentric, full of oneself
Sensational	Unimpressive, ordinary
Sensible	Nonsensical, moronic
Sensitive	Unfeeling, closed
Sensual	Cold, stiff
Set	Flexible, bending
Sexy	Plain, unattractive
Shaky	Steady, calm, stable
Sharp	Dull, unintelligent, idiotic
Sheltered	Exposed, worldly
Shining	Dull, faded, foggy
Shiny	Graying, dull
Short-tempered	Patient, agreeable
Shrewd	Unintelligent, dull-witted
Shy	Bold, outspoken, extraverted
Sick	Healthy, well, vibrant
Significant	Unimportant, worthless, unvalued
Silent	Exuberant, loud, wordy
Simple	Elegant, extravagant, fancy
Sleepy	Alert, revived, awake
Sluggish	Energetic, excited
Small	Big, gigantic, abnormous, huge
Smart	Dumb, stupid
Smiley	Frowny
Smooth	Rough, hairy, bumpy
Smug	Insecure, unconfident
Snug	Cold, fishy, clammy
Sophisticated	Unglamorous, lackluster
Sore	Strong, pumped
Sorrowful	Joyful, innocent
Sought	Unwanted, undesired
Special	Ordinary, average
Speechless	Babbling, gabby, chatty
Spent	Energized, rejuvenated, refreshed
Spicy	Plain, mild, simple
Spirited	Empty, unfulfilled
Splendid	Lacking, drab
Spontaneous	Planned, scheduled, organized
Stable	Crazy, unpredictable, shaky
Stagnant	Active, stirred
Starving	Satisfied, full
Static	Changing, evolving, moving
Stationary	Still, static, unmoving
Steadfast	Disloyal, unfaithful, unreliable

Stiff	Flexible, moveable
Still	Active, jittery
Stimulated	Bored, uninterested, turned off
Stinky	Fragrant, fresh
Stirred	Unmoved, still, unchanging
Strained	Relaxed, calm, at ease
Strange	Similar, known, common
Stressed	Relaxed, peaceful
Stretched	Unchanged, unreformed
Striving	Content
Strong	Weak, lacking, small
Strong-minded	Timid, dispirited
Stubborn	Agreeable, giving, submissive
Stuck	Unaffected, remiss
Stuffed	Hungry, ravenous
Stunning	Plain, unimpressive
Stylish	Out-of-date, unfashionable
Suggestive	Hidden, obscured, incognito
Sulky	Jubilant, upbeat
Super	Ordinary, plain, common
Superb	Crude, average, meek
Superior	Inferior, lowly
Supported	Neglected, isolated, an island
Supportive	Antagonistic, villainous
Surprised	Expectant
Surprising	Predictable, expected
Surrendered	Feisty, rebellious, making a stand
Suspicious	Unsuspecting
Swamped	Keeping up, underwhelmed
Sweet	Cruel, hard, cold, uncaring
Swollen	Elegant, well-shaped
Sympathetic	Unmoved, uncaring, apathetic
Taciturn	Fluent, babbling, talkative
Targeted	Unfounded, unmarked
Taxed	Energized
Temperamental	Stable, steady, even-keeled
Tenacious	Lazy, lackadaisical, laid back
Tender	Hard-hearted, coarse
Tense	Loose, flexible
Terrific	Awful, horrible
Thankful	Ungrateful, unappreciative
Thirsty	Quenched, full, hydrated
Thoughtful	Thoughtless, uncaring, uncompassionate
Thrilled	Bored, uninterested, dulled

Tight	Loose, flexible, open
Timely	Late, tardy, behind
Timid	Bold, daring, adventurous
Tired	Alert, awake, engaged
Toasted	Sober, straight
Toasty	Frigid, cold, freezing
Touching	Uninspiring, unmoving
Tranquil	Excitable, exhilarating
Transfixed	Wandering, drifting, aimless
Transformed	Unchanged
Transforming	Inflexible
Transparent	Opaque, dishonest, blocked
Traumatized	Delighted, soothed, at ease
Treasured	Neglected, left alone, devalued
Tremendous	Ordinary, average
Trendy	Out-of-style, dated
Troubled	Relaxed, unworried, pleased
Trusted	Suspect, wary
Trustful	Suspicious
Trusting	Doubtful, watching
Trustworthy	Incredulous, dubious
Turgid	Modest, simple, reserved
Unbelievable	Realistic, imaginable, likely
Uncertain	Assured, confident, positive
Unchanging	Evolving, flexing, bending
Uncomfortable	Cozy, tucked in, at ease
Understood	Misunderstood, misconceived, wrong
Undervalued	Treasured, cherished, worthy
Undisturbed	Messed up, cluttered
Uneasy	Restful, at ease, aligned
Unfocused	Engaged, engrossed, absorbed
Unhappy	Content, joyous, blissful
Unimportant	Significant, honored, respected, worshipped
Unique	Ordinary, average, run-of-the-mill
Unpredictable	Planned, scheduled, expected
Unprepared	Skilled, trained, educated, ready
Unrecognizable	Known, recognized, conspicuous, caught
Unrelenting	Surrendered, submissive, agreeable
Unruffled	Frantic, feathered
Unsettled	Calm, relaxed
Unshakable	Jittery, fidgety, unsettled
Unstable	Steady, strong
Unsteady	Balanced, strong
Unsure	Certain, assured, confident

Untiring	Exhausted, worn out, run down
Unwanted	Desired, coveted, sought
Unwearied	Tired, drained, wiped out
Upset	Unaffected, relaxed, at ease
Used	Needed, appreciated
Useful	Taken for granted, meaningless, insignificant
Valiant	Cowardly, weak, timid
Valuable	Unworthy, ignored, unimportant
Vehement	Blasé, nonchalant, apathetic
Victorious	Beaten, defeated, deflated
Vigilant	Oblivious, neglectful, remiss
Virtuous	Sleazy, easy, loose
Vital	Unnecessary, unneeded, frivolous
Vivacious	Worn, decaying
Volatile	Mild-mannered, agreeable
Voracious	Dispassionate
Vulnerable	Closed, private, unsharing
Wanted	Undesirable, ignored
Wanting	Dismissing, ignoring, rejecting, turning away
Warm	Cold, cool, disconnected
Watchful	Negligent, ignorant, unobservant
Weak	Strong, bulky, pumped up, fit
Weary	Alert, revived, awake, replenished
Wise	Dull-witted, unintelligent, not-the-brightest-bulb-in-the-pack
Wistful	Logical, realistic, likely
Withdrawn	Engaged, extraverted, open
Withered	Glowing, thriving, vibrant
Woeful	Excited, upbeat, optimistic, hopeful
Wonderful	Unimpressive, average, normal
Woozy	Fresh, steady, healthy, well
Wordy	Quiet, shy, withdrawn, reserved
Worldly	Sheltered, protected, innocent, naïve
Worn	Energized, vital, vivacious
Worried	Relaxed, unconcerned, prayerful
Worthwhile	Unnecessary, ridiculous, futile
Worthy	Worthless, unimportant, insignificant
Wounded	Healed, mended, healthy, well
Wowed	Uninterested, bored, unimpressed
Wretched	Cheerful, encouraging, comforting
Yearning	Releasing, unwanted
Young	Old, worn, decrepit
Zealous	Procrastinating . . . but, you don't have to, anymore! Here's the rest of your Experimental Word Playing!

Word

Word Play!

Play

Word Play!

Word

Play

Play

Word

Word Play!

WORD PLAY . . . YOUR Upside-Downed Verbal Emojis

Your turn again! Just as with the dictionary and thesaurus, let's not forget about YOUR Verbal Emojis. Create your own upside-downed words and phrases for your own verbal emojis list.

Here's where it can get really fun. Think about each of your verbal emojis and try to decide whether the word or phrase is related to a thought, feeling, or imagining. Let's get back to our word "patient" used as your bonus 705th Verbal Emoji. In using the upside-downed words and phrases, let's say you have a character waiting at home who is anything but patient. Adding introspection could change the word choice for an emotion (verbal emoji). For instance, your character could be pensive (in thought), concerned (in feelings), or worried (imagining or picturing a negative outcome) while waiting for a loved one to return home in a snow storm.

Think also about the time of day in relation to your verbal emoji as how a feeling is expressed when refreshed, when washing off the work of the day, and when exhausted at night could be three different things. Note that these considerations are also used in Volume 1 of the Experimental Word Player series, **500+ Happenings to Prove Existence***!*

WORD OR PHRASE	~~ANTONYMS~~ UPSIDE-DOWNED VERBAL EMOJIS

WORD OR PHRASE	~~ANTONYMS~~ UPSIDE-DOWNED VERBAL EMOJIS

64

WORD OR PHRASE	~~ANTONYMS~~ UPSIDE-DOWNED VERBAL EMOJIS

WORD OR PHRASE	~~ANTONYMS~~ UPSIDE-DOWNED VERBAL EMOJIS

WORD OR PHRASE	~~ANTONYMS~~ UPSIDE-DOWNED VERBAL EMOJIS

WORD OR PHRASE	~~ANTONYMS~~ UPSIDE-DOWNED VERBAL EMOJIS

Categories

VERBAL

VERBAL

Emojis

Categories

Verbal

Emojis

Emojis

CATEGORIES

69

WORD PLAY . . . *Verbal Emojis Categories*

There's more than one way to skin a cat and there're more than a couple ways to organize a thesaurus. Those organizational choices go well beyond the definitions, synonyms, and anonyms of a word.

For reals now! How many times have you looked in a thesaurus, or quick hit <shift>+<F7>, just to realize that the word you were looking up (which maybe didn't have exactly the right feel) was not the right word AT ALL?

There are no suitable synonyms for your word. It would be great if the thesaurus or the <shift>+<F7> feature could provide a couple of other alternatives that were in the same ballpark.

To all of you who thought thesauruses needed a make-over, here are the verbal emojis categories.

On a basic level, all emotions can be categorized as positive, negative or neutral. Positive emotions are those that generally make you feel good, or make a reader feel good while reading. BUBBLING OVER! Negative emotions are those that generally make you feel bad, or make a reader feel bad while reading. BOILING OVER! Neutral emotions don't make anyone feel much of anything one way or another, but may be relatable. ANTICIPATING.

Or what about JOYFUL, versus SATISFIED, versus CONTENT? Three totally different feels for the generic verbal emoji, HAPPY.

Adding a positive, negative, or neutral categorization of your verbal emojis can be helpful to determining which synonyms and antonyms to use when, based on the moment, mood, or temperament of your character!

What's that? Oh, yeah; you're right. Some verbal emojis can fall into more than one—or even all three—categories. That's been accounted for. No worries.

Positive Verbal Emojis

Absorbed
Absorbing
Active
Active
Admired
Adorable
Adored
Adroit
Adventurous
Affectionate
Affirmed
Affluent
Ahead
Alert
Alive
Alluring
Altruistic
Amatory
Amazed
Amazing
Ambitious
Animated
Anticipatory
Appreciated
Appreciative
Aroused
Artistic
Assiduous
Astonishing
Astounded
Astounding
Attentive
Attractive
Audacious
Avid
Awakened
Awed
Awe-inspiring
Awesome
Bashful
Beautiful
Beloved

Bewitching
Big
Blessed
Blissful
Bold
Bouncy
Brainy
Brave
Breathtaking
Bright
Brilliant
Bubbly
Busy
Candid
Capable
Carefree
Caring
Casual
Certain
Changing
Charmed
Charming
Chaste
Cheerful
Cheerful
Cheery
Cherished
Chic
Childish
Clean
Clever
Collected
Colossal
Comely
Comfortable
Comforting
Commendable
Compassionate
Complex
Complicated
Composed
Concerned

Confident
Consumed
Contemplative
Content
Cool
Courageous
Coveted
Cozy
Crafty
Creative
Curvaceous
Daring
Dazzling
Decisive
Delicate
Delighted
Dependable
Desired
Determined
Difficult
Diplomatic
Disbelieving
Distinctive
Dizzy
Docile
Dramatic
Dreaming
Dreamy
Driving
Dry
Eager
Earnest
Easygoing
Ebullient
Ecstatic
Edgy
Effervescent
Emotional
Empowered
Empowering
Empty
Encouraged
Encouraging
Energized

Engaged
Engrossed
Enjoyable
Enlivened
Enthralling
Enthusiastic
Enticing
Equipped
Erotic
Esteemed
Estimable
Evolving
Exalted
Excellent
Exceptional
Excited
Exhausted
Expanded
Expanding
Expectant
Experienced
Expressive
Exquisite
Extraordinary
Extroverted
Exultant
Fabulous
Famous
Fantastic
Fascinated
Fascinating
Fashionable
Favored
Fearless
Fervent
Fiery
Fine
Firm
Flabbergasted
Flattered
Floppy
Flummoxed
Flushed
Focused

Foreign
Fortunate
Fragile
Free
Fresh
Friendly
Frisky
Fulfilled
Full
Functional
Funny
Generous
Gentle
Gigantic
Glad
Gorgeous
Grand
Grateful
Gratified
Great
Growing
Gutsy
Hairy
Happy
Hardened
Hard-working
Harmless
Heavy
Heroic
Hidden
Hilarious
Hip
Honest
Honored
Hopeful
Hormonal
Hot
Huge
Humble
Hungry
Ideal
Illecebrous
Important
Impressed

Impressive
Impulsive
Incredible
Inflated
Influential
Inquisitive
Insistent
Inspired
Inspiring
Instinctive
Intelligent
Interested
Interesting
Intrigued
Intriguing
Intuitive
Irreplaceable
Jolly
Jovial
Joyful
Joyous
Judicious
Keen
Kept
Kind
Kindhearted
Lackadaisical
Laudable
Lazy
Lively
Logical
Longing
Loquacious
Loved
Lovely
Loving
Lucky
Magical
Majestic
Marked
Marvelous
Massive
Matchless
Mature

Meditative

Meek

Mellow

Memorable

Mesmerizing

Mesmerizing

Methodical

Mind-blowing

Mindful

Miraculous

Mischievous

Modest

Monstrous

Motivated

Mysterious

Naïve

Natural

Naughty

Needed

Nervous

Notable

Noticed

Odd

OK

Old

Open

Ordinary

Organized

Orgasmic

Outgoing

Outspoken

Outstanding

Overawed

Overcome

Overwhelmed

Overwhelming

Particular

Passionate

Patient

Peaceful

Peachy

Peppy

Perceptive

Perfect

Perplexed

Persevering

Persistent

Phenomenal

Pious

Playful

Pleased

Plucky

Poised

Positive

Powerful

Practical

Praiseworthy

Prayerful

Precious

Precious

Predictable

Prepared

Primed

Privileged

Prized

Protected

Protective

Proud

Puffy

Purposeful

Puzzled

Puzzling

Questioning

Quick

Quiet

Racy

Randy

Rare

Rational

Ravenous

Ready

Receptive

Recognizable

Refreshed

Rejuvenated

Relaxed

Reliable

Relieved

Relished
Remarkable
Renewed
Resolute
Respected
Responsive
Rested
Restful
Revived
Rewarded
Rich
Risky
Riveted
Riveting
Rushed
Sacred
Safe
Sagacious
Sane
Sarcastic
Sassy
Satisfied
Secure
Seeking
Seen
Selfless
Sensational
Sensible
Sensitive
Sensual
Set
Sexy
Sharp
Sheltered
Shining
Shiny
Shrewd
Shy
Significant
Silent
Simple
Sleepy
Small
Smart

Smiley
Smooth
Smug
Snug
Sophisticated
Sought
Special
Speechless
Spent
Spicy
Spirited
Splendid
Spontaneous
Stable
Starving
Static
Stationary
Steadfast
Stiff
Still
Stimulated
Stirred
Strange
Stretched
Striving
Strong
Strong-minded
Stuffed
Stunning
Stylish
Suggestive
Super
Superb
Superior
Supported
Supportive
Surprised
Surprising
Suspicious
Swamped
Sweet
Swollen
Sympathetic
Taciturn

Targeted
Tenacious
Tender
Terrific
Thankful
Thirsty
Thoughtful
Thrilled
Timely
Timid
Tired
Toasty
Touching
Tranquil
Transfixed
Transformed
Transforming
Treasured
Tremendous
Trendy
Trusted
Trustful
Trusting
Trustworthy
Unbelievable
Unchanging
Understood
Undisturbed
Unique
Unpredictable
Unrecognizable
Unrelenting

Unruffled
Unshakable
Untiring
Unwearied
Useful
Valiant
Valuable
Vehement
Victorious
Vigilant
Virtuous
Vital
Vivacious
Volatile
Voracious
Wanted
Wanting
Warm
Watchful
Wise
Wistful
Wonderful
Wordy
Worldly
Worn
Worthwhile
Worthy
Wowed
Yearning
Young
Zealous

Negative Verbal Emojis

Abnormous
Absent
Absorbed
Absorbing
Absurd
Achy
Adrift
Aggressive
Agitated
Alienated
Amazed
Ambitious
Angry
Animated
Annoyed
Anticipatory
Antiquated
Antsy
Anxious
Apathetic
Apprehensive
Ashamed
Astonishing
Astounded
Astounding
Audacious
Avid
Awakened
Awed
Awkward
Bashful
Beaten
Behind
Besieged
Bewitching
Big
Bitter
Blasé
Bloated
Blue
Bogglish
Bold

Bored
Boring
Bossy
Bouncy
Bulging
Busy
Candid
Casual
Certain
Changing
Chaste
Childish
Claustrophobic
Clean
Clever
Clingy
Closed
Cold
Colossal
Complex
Complicated
Concerned
Confident
Confused
Constrained
Consumed
Contemplative
Cool
Coveted
Cowardly
Creepy
Crushed
Curvaceous
Cynical
Damaged
Decisive
Dehydrated
Dejected
Delayed
Delicate
Depleted
Depressed

Desolate

Difficult

Disbelieving

Dissatisfied

Distended

Distracted

Distressed

Distrustful

Disturbed

Dizzy

Docile

Doubtful

Dowdy

Down

Drained

Dramatic

Dreaming

Driving

Drowsy

Dry

Dubious

Dull

Eager

Edgy

Effervescent

Egocentric

Egotistic

Embarrassed

Emotional

Empty

Engorged

Engrossed

Enraged

Enticing

Erratic

Estranged

Evolving

Exhausted

Expanded

Expanding

Expectant

Explosive

Exposed

Extroverted

Faint

Fake

Fat

Fatigued

Fearful

Feeble

Fervent

Fiery

Firm

Flabbergasted

Floppy

Flummoxed

Flushed

Foggy

Foreign

Forgetful

Forlorn

Fragile

Frail

Frantic

Fraught

Frazzled

Free

Frightened

Full

Funny

Gentle

Gigantic

Gloomy

Glum

Greedy

Groggy

Growing

Guilty

Gutsy

Hairy

Hardened

Harmless

Hassled

Haunted

Heavy

Hesitant

Hidden

Hilarious

Hip
Hollow
Hormonal
Hot
Hubristic
Huge
Humble
Hungry
Hunted
Hurried
Hurt
Ill
Illogical
Immature
Impatient
Imperfect
Imperious
Impious
Impish
Impish
Impressed
Impressive
Impulsive
Indecisive
Inflated
Infuriated
Inquisitive
Insane
Insecure
Insignificant
Insistent
Insomniatic
Instinctive
Interrupted
Intrigued
Intriguing
Introverted
Intuitive
Inundated
Irksome
Irrational
Irreplaceable
Irritable
Itchy

Jittery
Judicious
Keen
Kept
Lackadaisical
Lacking
Lamenting
Late
Lazy
Lethargic
Lewd
Livid
Longing
Loquacious
Lost
Lost
Marginalized
Marked
Massive
Matchless
Mediocre
Meek
Mellow
Mesmerizing
Mesmerizing
Messy
Methodical
Mind-blowing
Mischievous
Miserable
Misguided
Misjudged
Misunderstood
Modest
Monstrous
Moody
Morose
Mysterious
Naïve
Naughty
Nauseous
Needed
Needy
Needy

Neglected	Quick
Nervous	Quiet
Notable	Racy
Noticed	Randy
Oblivious	Rare
Obtuse	Rational
Odd	Ravenous
OK	Recognizable
Old	Regretful
Open	Relaxed
Ordinary	Resigned
Outspoken	Resolute
Overawed	Risky
Overcome	Riveted
Overextended	Riveting
Overwhelmed	Rude
Overwhelming	Ruffled
Parched	Rushed
Particular	Sacred
Pathetic	Sad
Perplexed	Sarcastic
Persistent	Sassy
Picky	Scared
Pious	Scarred
Poised	Scrawny
Poor	Seeking
Powerful	Seen
Practical	Selfish
Prayerful	Sensitive
Precious	Sensual
Precious	Sexy
Predictable	Shaky
Preoccupied	Sharp
Protected	Sheltered
Protective	Short-tempered
Proud	Shy
Puffy	Sick
Purposeful	Silent
Pushy	Simple
Puzzled	Sleepy
Puzzling	Sluggish
Queasy	Small
Querulous	Smug
Questioning	Sore

Sorrowful
Sought
Speechless
Spent
Spicy
Spontaneous
Stagnant
Starving
Static
Stationary
Stiff
Still
Stimulated
Stinky
Stirred
Strained
Strange
Stressed
Stretched
Stubborn
Stuck
Stuffed
Suggestive
Sulky
Surprised
Surprising
Suspicious
Swamped
Swollen
Taciturn
Targeted
Taxed
Temperamental
Tenacious
Tender
Tense
Thirsty
Thrilled
Tight
Timid
Tired
Toasted
Toasty
Transfixed

Transformed
Transforming
Transparent
Traumatized
Troubled
Trusting
Turgid
Unbelievable
Uncertain
Unchanging
Uncomfortable
Undervalued
Uneasy
Unfocused
Unhappy
Unimportant
Unpredictable
Unprepared
Unrecognizable
Unrelenting
Unsettled
Unstable
Unsteady
Unsure
Untiring
Unwanted
Upset
Used
Vehement
Vital
Volatile
Voracious
Vulnerable
Wanting
Warm
Watchful
Weak
Weary
Withdrawn
Withered
Woeful
Woozy
Wordy
Worldly

Worn
Worried
Wounded
Wowed

Wretched
Yearning
Young

Neutral Verbal Emojis

Absent	Empty
Absorbed	Equipped
Absorbing	Exhausted
Active	Expanded
Active	Expanding
Adrift	Expectant
Adventurous	Expressive
Agreeable	Faint
Ahead	Fine
Alert	Floppy
Alive	Fragile
Altruistic	Free
Ambitious	Full
Antiquated	Functional
Apathetic	Gentle
Articulate	Growing
Artistic	Hairy
Awake	Hardened
Awakened	Harmless
Aware	Hollow
Awkward	Hormonal
Behind	Huge
Big	Hungry
Blasé	Instinctive
Bloated	Introverted
Brainy	Intuitive
Bulging	Lackadaisical
Calm	Logical
Carefree	Mediocre
Casual	Meditative
Certain	Meek
Clean	Mellow
Closed	Memorable
Colossal	Methodical
Comfortable	Modest
Concerned	OK
Content	Practical
Cool	Predictable
Delayed	Prepared
Distracted	Primed
Dreaming	Puffy
Dry	Quiet

Ravenous
Relaxed
Resolute
Responsive
Rested
Restful
Seen
Shining
Shiny
Silent
Simple
Sleepy
Small
Smooth
Snug
Stable
Static
Stationary

Steadfast
Stiff
Still
Stirred
Stretched
Stuffed
Targeted
Tender
Thirsty
Thoughtful
Tired
Toasty
Warm
Watchful
Wordy
Worldly
Young

Word
Word Play!
Play
Word Play!
Word
Play
Play

Word
WORD PLAY!

85

WORD PLAY . . . YOUR Verbal Emojis Categories

Your turn! Make a list of POSITIVE/NEGATIVE/NEUTRAL *verbal emojis based on your own verbal emojis list. Remember, some words may be on more than one list.*

POSITIVE	NEGATIVE	NEUTRAL

POSITIVE	NEGATIVE	NEUTRAL

POSITIVE	NEGATIVE	NEUTRAL

Emojis

Temperances

TEMPERANCES

VERBAL

Emojis

Temperances

Verbal

Emojis

Verbal

Verbal Emojis Temperances

Okay, so technically "temperances" is not a word, but seeing as we're in the business of making words, and finding right words, I thought you might let it go this time. Temperature is about hot and cold and that is accurate for our next manner of sorting out this not-so-little list of ours. However, temperance is about moderation and control of one's mood, emotions, and natural character or reaction. It is really both of these things that are necessary to fully drill down on how to best use our verbal emojis.

In addition to finding the right verbal emoji to express your characters' thoughts, feelings, and imaginings, it is important to make sure the verbal emoji is as strong as the expression being experienced. What is its **temperature**? *Then,* **moderate** *it to your character. Temperatures plus temperance equals our made up "temperances".*

What do I mean by that?

Emotions have energy. Emotions have flavors and strength. That's one of the benefits of the yellow smiley emojis, right? Some are simply stationary smiling faces. Others are smiling faces with blushing cheeks, or rolling eyes, or a wink, or any other handful of animations. Each face expresses happiness, but to a different degree . . . a different temperature. Each has its own temperance.

As writers, we are typically confined to the stationary black and white type on a page, so animated characters and gifs are not really in our writing vocabulary. Verbal emojis can be used, though, to get the same range of energy, flavor, or strength from a given emotion.

That's why a verbal emoji choice is so important. Choosing the wrong verbal emoji can cause your character to over- or under-react. Or perhaps choosing the right verbal emoji can cause your character to over- or under-react. Either way, selection of the proper verbal emoji is key and using the right temperature emoji creates the proper temperance of the scene or moment you are trying to create.

Also, don't confuse extremity with negativity. Temperance is different than the positive, negative, and neutral categorization. To demonstrate, I've actually created temperance sentences for all three categories of verbal emojis!

Perhaps this one is better understood in example. I give you verbal emojis temperances! Five each of positive, negative, and neutral verbal emojis are broken down into sample sentences that are cool or cold, to warm or room temperature, to hot. Take a look for yourself and grow the temperance practice through some of your own miniature word plays.

Positive

Check out these five positive verbal emojis reflected in different temperances.

HAPPY/DELIGHTED/JOVIAL

The sunshine made her *happy* after the three-day rain spell.

She was *delighted* to see her family over Christmas break after being away at school since September.

The news she was going to be an aunt made her downright *jovial* and she couldn't contain her excitement.

Just an itty bitty experimental word play . . . Think about other words that could mean "happy" (I'm pretty sure you can find a few in this list); what is the temperance of the word you chose and how might you use it in your writing?

_____

_____

_____

LOVED/CHERISHED/ADORED

She lay down in bed and snuggled next to him, silently thanking God for giving her a partner who made her feel so *loved*.

He had a picture of her in his wallet. The gesture left her feeling *cherished*.

Her desk was covered with flowers, chocolates, cards and gifts on her birthday. Clearly someone *adored* her, but did he have to be so extravagant about it?

Just an itty bitty experimental word play . . . Think about other words that could mean "loved" (I'm pretty sure you can find a few in this list); what is the temperance of the word you chose and how might you use it in your writing?

_____

_____

_____

FOCUSED/ENGROSSED/ABSORBED

He was *focused* despite the noise in the background.

I was so *engrossed* in my work that I missed lunch.

She was so *absorbed* in her work that hours, days passed without her thinking about anything else.

Just an itty bitty experimental word play . . . Think about other words that could mean "focused" (I'm pretty sure you can find a few in this list); what is the temperance of the word you chose and how might you use it in your writing?

_____

_____

_____

BUBBLY/EFFERVESCENT/VIVACIOUS

The children were expectantly *bubbly* on the bus and chatted excitedly on the way to the zoo.

The sweet young girl was as *effervescent* as the champagne in her glass and she chatted merrily with every gentleman who gave her a moment of attention.

She was the most *vivacious* one in the group. I could hear her from across the room despite the crowd and, every once in awhile, I could catch her arms gesturing wildly to keep pace with the passion in her voice.

Just an itty bitty experimental word play . . . Think about other words that could mean "bubbly" (I'm pretty sure you can find a few in this list); what is the temperance of the word you chose and how might you use it in your writing?

_____

_____

_____

PLUCKY/BOLD/COURAGEOUS

The girl was a known bully and I didn't want any trouble. If it was up to me, I would have just picked my books off the ground and walked quickly away. My friend, however, is *plucky* and walked right up to her and told her off.

Challenging the professor in front of the whole class was a bold move, but he was a *bold* guy and not afraid to stand up especially when he thought he was in the right.

She was scared to walk into that room knowing the situation, but that's what made her *courageous*. She did what she had to do anyway.

Just an itty bitty experimental word play . . . Think about other words that could mean "plucky" (I'm pretty sure you can find a few in this list); what is the temperance of the word you chose and how might you use it in your writing?

_____

_____

_____

<u>Negative</u>

Check out these five negative verbal emojis reflected in different temperances.

BUSY/SWAMPED/OVERWHELMED

Between school and work, she certainly was busy.

She looked at her schedule for the day. Back-to-back meetings in the morning and a conference call in the afternoon. Add to that the list of call she needed to make and the ever increasing number of emails in her inbox and she felt just **swamped**.

He was trying to do it all and felt ***overwhelmed*** just thinking about it. It's impossible to do everything and be everybody.

Just an itty bitty experimental word play . . . Think about other words that could mean "busy" (I'm pretty sure you can find a few in this list); what is the temperance of the word you chose and how might you use it in your writing?

_____

_____

_____

BLOATED/SWOLLEN/TURGID

The burritos for lunch left her feeling **bloated**.

Her shoes were so tight her feet looked **swollen**.

She looked at herself in the mirror and, at exactly forty weeks pregnant, she felt ***turgid***. Her skin was pulled tight across her belly. She was retaining water and her legs looked like sausage casings ready to burst. She was ready to be done.

Just an itty bitty experimental word play . . . Think about other words that could mean "bloated" (I'm pretty sure you can find a few in this list); what is the temperance of the word you chose and how might you use it in your writing?

_____

_____

_____

SMALL/UNIMPORTANT/INSIGNIFICANT

She felt *small* standing among the other basketball players.

Looking at the other titles in the room she felt decidedly *unimportant*. She was not a CEO, or CTO, or president or owner of anything.

The view was magnificent. The mountains towered majestically making the voids between peaks seem infinite and timeless. The perspective made her feel *insignificant*.

Just an itty bitty experimental word play . . . Think about other words that could mean "small" (I'm pretty sure you can find a few in this list); what is the temperance of the word you chose and how might you use it in your writing?

_____

_____

_____

HUNGRY/STARVING/VORACIOUS

She was *hungry*, so she ate a sandwich.

She was *starving* and couldn't settle for just a sandwich. She ate the chips and cookie too!

She was just leaving work and hadn't eaten since breakfast. She ransacked her purse on the way to the car and found a granola bar. She was **voracious** and ripped into the wrapper with her teeth the moment she sat down.

Just an itty bitty experimental word play . . . Think about other words that could mean "hungry" (I'm pretty sure you can find a few in this list); what is the temperance of the word you chose and how might you use it in your writing?

_____

_____

_____

ANNOYED/ANGRY/LIVID

I was **annoyed** by the third month of construction outside my window.

She was so **angry** she could have spit nails. How could he have forgotten their anniversary . . . AGAIN?

This was the fifth time in a row he left her waiting alone at the restaurant without warning. She was **livid**. It will take more than fancy dinner with flowers and a bottle of wine to apologize this time.

Just an itty bitty experimental word play . . . Think about other words that could mean "annoyed" (I'm pretty sure you can find a few in this list); what is the temperance of the word you chose and how might you use it in your writing?

_____

_____

_____

Neutral

Check out these five positive verbal emojis reflected in different temperances.

DROWSY/TIRED/EXHAUSTED

I was starting to feel *drowsy* after cleaning up dinner, but my book was there on the coffee table just calling to me.

He was *tired* after working twelve hour shifts three days in a row.

She was up early the day before to get a quick workout in, and she had been up half the night with a sick child. To say she was *exhausted* was an understatement. She just hoped she didn't fall asleep during the meeting.

Just an itty bitty experimental word play . . . Think about other words that could mean "drowsy" (I'm pretty sure you can find a few in this list); what is the temperance of the word you chose and how might you use it in your writing?

_____

_____

_____

BLASÉ/CAREFREE/OBLIVIOUS

His *blasé* mood matched the weather. It wasn't hot out and it wasn't cold. It wasn't humid but it wasn't dry either.

If he would have checked the weather, he would have seen that it was going to rain, but he was too *carefree* to think of such things and headed to the festival anyway.

She walked home from the theater alone that night, completely *oblivious* to the neighborhood she had to walk through and the reputation of the area.

Just an itty bitty experimental word play . . . Think about other words that could mean "blasé" (I'm pretty sure you can find a few in this list); what is the temperance of the word you chose and how might you use it in your writing?

_____

_____

_____

CLEVER/ADROIT/SHREWD

My mom was *clever*, but not *clever* enough. I knew there was a surprise party waiting for me inside but acted surprised anyway.

I watched the *adroit* boy across the table. He had all the mind teasers solved before I had worked out the first one.

He was *shrewd* enough to elude police for the third time. There were no fingerprints left at the scene, investigators were unable to recover any DNA from the cigarette butts found at the scene, and the security cameras somehow malfunctioned yet again.

Just an itty bitty experimental word play . . . Think about other words that could mean "clever" (I'm pretty sure you can find a few in this list); what is the temperance of the word you chose and how might you use it in your writing?

_____

_____

_____

DOWDY/OLD/ANTIQUATED

She felt *dowdy* wearing last year's fashion to the theater.

I took a tour of my alma mater's campus. Everything was changed and it made me feel *old*.

He paused in the middle of his conversation and looked at the phone in his hand. There was a cord connected to it. His daughter was laughing with a girl friend on her iPhone®. His wife was texting his son. And he was ordering pizza with a landline using a phone that was tethered to the wall. Boy did he feel *antiquated*.

Just an itty bitty experimental word play . . . Think about other words that could mean "dowdy" (I'm pretty sure you can find a few in this list); what is the temperance of the word you chose and how might you use it in your writing?

_____

_____

_____

TEMPERAMENTAL/MOODY/HORMONAL

It was rumored he was *temperamental* today, but he was in good spirits when I showed up. I still chose my words carefully, though, so as not to tip the scale.

The combination of tired and hungry left me feeling *moody*. I could be in a good mood one second and just the smallest things seemed to set me off.

He could always tell what was going on and he felt powerless to it. Once a month, like clockwork, she was a *hormonal* wreck. She would go from smiling to crying in a matter of seconds. The trendy outfit she put on that morning would feel uncomfortable and unflattering by noon.

Just an itty bitty experimental word play . . . Think about other words that could mean "temperamental" (I'm pretty sure you can find a few in this list); what is the temperance of the word you chose and how might you use it in your writing?

_____

_____

_____

Word
Word Play!
Play
Word Play!
Word
Play
Play

Word
WORD PLAY!

100

WORD PLAY . . . YOUR Verbal Emojis Temperances

Pick another positive verbal emoji from the list to break down into cool/cold, warm/room temperature, and hot sentences.

WORD:_____

Cool Sentence (and word):

_____

_____

Warm Sentence (and word):

_____

_____

Hot Sentence (and word):

_____

_____

How is the word or phrase different at its different temperances?

_____

_____

_____

Pick one of your own positive verbal emojis from your brainstormed (added) list to break down into cool/cold, warm/room temperature, and hot sentences.

WORD:_____

Cool Sentence (and word):

_____

_____

Warm Sentence (and word):

_____

_____

Hot Sentence (and word):

_____

_____

How is your word or phrase different at its different temperances?

_____

_____

_____

Pick another negative verbal emoji from the list to break down into cool/cold, warm/room temperature, and hot sentences.

WORD:_____

Cool Sentence (and word):

_____

_____

Warm Sentence (and word):

_____

_____

Hot Sentence (and word):

_____

_____

How is the word or phrase different at its different temperances?

_____

_____

_____

Pick one of your own negative verbal emojis from your brainstormed (added) list to break down into cool/cold, warm/room temperature, and hot sentences.

WORD:_____

Cool Sentence (and word):

_____

_____

Warm Sentence (and word):

_____

_____

Hot Sentence (and word):

_____

_____

How is your word or phrase different at its different temperances?

_____

_____

_____

Pick another neutral verbal emoji from the list to break down into cool/cold, warm/room temperature, and hot sentences.

WORD:_____

Cool Sentence (and word):

_____

_____

Warm Sentence (and word):

_____

_____

Hot Sentence (and word):

_____

_____

How is the word or phrase different at its different temperances?

_____

_____

_____

Pick one of your own neutral verbal emojis from your brainstormed (added) list to break down into cool/cold, warm/room temperature, and hot sentences.

WORD:_____

Cool Sentence (and word):

_____

_____

Warm Sentence (and word):

_____

_____

Hot Sentence (and word):

_____

_____

How is your word or phrase different at its different temperances?

_____

_____

_____

Characterizations

VERBAL

VERBAL

Emojis

Characterizations

Verbal

Emojis

CHARACTERIZATIONS

Emojis

Verbal Emojis Characterizations

Verbal emojis tell a lot about a character. Aside from the obvious how your character is feeling at a given moment, verbal emojis contain significant secondary meanings. A reader can look at the character's emotion and understand why a character behaves a certain way, predict what a character is going to do, and empathize with the character's reactions. Verbal emojis don't just solidify a character; they help create sustainable, relatable, memorable humans (okay, and—depending on your story—animals and other personified stars of your stories).

You can also use verbal emojis to convey the depth of a character when the character's actions may be otherwise limited. A character, even when not moving or acted upon by outside forces, still has active internal forces.

So there.

Instead of painting a character with big yellow cartoon faces, give the verbal emojis a try.

Check out how these ten passages use a verbal emoji to convey the depth of a character.

AMBITIOUS

Positive Passage

He's may be a guy, but that's not a guarantee for earning jobs, anymore. She's ambitious. She takes charge. She did the work . . . every day. She deserves the promotion.

Negative Passage

He was competitive and ambitious, and in him those two qualities formed a natural inclination to take advantage of opportunities as they presented. So he couldn't resist peaking over his shoulder at the neighboring desk when the teacher left the room.

Neutral Passage

The hotel's style was an ambitious juxtaposition of old-English hunting lodge and modern world traveler.

EXPECTANT

Positive Passage

Just two days past due and she lay in bed fixating on every little twinge with expectant anticipation. The hospital bag had been packed for weeks now.

Negative Passage

I sat with my door closed - expectant of the footsteps that inevitable approach at 4:55 P.M. with an urgent assignment.

Neutral Passage

He put the cover on the patio furniture, expectant of the coming rain.

INSTINCTIVE

Positive Passage

I was never a dancer, but with him leading, I didn't need to worry. My movements were instinctive and directed his momentum.

Negative Passage

She was instinctive and knew better than to disregard the sick feeling forming in the pit of her stomach.

Neutral Passage

After three months of swimming in the morning, her breath control was instinctive and she could clear her mind.

LACKADAISICAL

Positive Passage

It was one of the best days ever. Sunshine, food and drink were abundant. She decided to simply enjoy herself and that moment and let someone else deal with the planning. What did it matter whether they all sat by the pool for the afternoon or stayed in the shade of the trees? Let the others scribble about the details she thought with a lackadaisical air.

Negative Passage

His lackadaisical approach to life created more and more stress as the deadlines approached. He needed to change.

Neutral Passage

As the nitrous oxide began to take effect, he became increasingly lackadaisical and let the dentist begin drilling without protest.

METHODICAL

Positive Passage

The instructions matched my methodical personality, so it took me barely any time to assemble the coffee table.

Negative Passage

The evidence indicated a truly methodical approach. The smaller items of highest value had been quickly taken while the larger items were left behind.

Neutral Passage

Her organization was methodical: coffee cup to the left of her computer along with her phone; she kept her pens to the right of the computer along with a notepad. She was right-handed, after all.

PRACTICAL

Positive Passage

He knew she was a keeper, but planning their wedding proved it. She was practical. She didn't need centerpieces that were five feet high and prevented guests from seeing one another and talking. She was happy with simple vases and a small arrangement to add elegance, but nothing too grand to distract from enjoying the company at the table.

Negative Passage

To him, certain activities were intended for procreation only, and he was too practical to deviate from that purpose.

Neutral Passage

She packed light - only taking her credit cards, phone, and chapstick. You could tell she was a practical person.

PREDICTABLE

Positive Passage

Her boss was predictable, making it easier to prepare for her review. She had answers to his questions ready before they were asked.

Negative Passage

It was always the same. He was so predictable. He never thought to try anything new and never wanted to even if it was suggested. It made life so boring.

Neutral Passage

She arrived five minutes early, as expected. She was so predictable.

RESOLUTE

Positive Passage

When she saw the way the restaurant owner turned the homeless man away, she stood up and demanded he be given a sandwich. She was resolute and even offered to pay twice the cost.

Negative Passage

Despite all his friends' protests, he still went ahead and planned a vacation with his girlfriend. He was resolute and there was no changing his mind.

Neutral Passage

Her kids wanted different foods for dinner again, as always. One wanted pizza, the other spaghetti. So she was resolute in her solution and made chicken.

STILL

Positive Passage

She loved her hour of yoga and meditation every morning. She walked out of the studio peaceful and still in spirit, ready to brace against the push of her crazy life.

Negative Passage

He walked into a quiet house and found her sitting next to the phone, completely still. He knew something was wrong.

Neutral Passage

She adopted the still of the early morning as she headed out that morning with her coffee.

WORLDLY

Positive Passage

Her worldly perspective allowed her to look past the shock of a toddler nursing in public and understand the natural and nurturing connection between mother and child.

Negative Passage

She was worldly and used it as an excuse for her seemingly experimental lifestyle.

Neutral Passage

Her company always sent her when there were meetings in foreign countries. She was worldly and the foreign sounds, smells and sights weren't offsetting to her.

Word

Word Play!

Play

Word Play!

Word

Play

Play

Word

Word Play!

Your Verbal Emojis Characterizations

Your turn to play! Pick one of your positive verbal emojis (or another from the list we provided) to create a passage that helps to create a strong character. Remember, the characterization does not have to be positive.

_____

_____

_____

_____

_____

_____

_____

_____

_____

_____

Your turn to play! Pick one of your negative verbal emojis (or another from the list we provided) to create a passage that helps to create a strong character. Remember, the characterization doesn't have to be negative.

Your turn to play! Pick one of your neutral verbal emojis (or another from the list we provided) to create a passage that helps to create a strong character. Remember, the characterization doesn't have to be neutral

---

at

VERBAL EMOJIS
Verbal Emojis

Work
VERBAL EMOJIS

at
Work

WORK

at

Verbal Emojis at Work

Sure, selecting one or two yellow circles from a predetermined collection of pre-canned emotional indicators is quick and easy, but you get what you pay for. A smiley-face (or frowny-face or "enter-other-generic-term"-face here) that reflects a small, narrow, stereotyped emotion that, like much of our language and humanity, is slowly being generalized from overuse.

Your characters deserve more than one of the pre-canned sentiments that society has decided is worthy enough to be assigned an emoticon.

Your characters are yours. Give them life! Give them the privilege of depth and complexity. Use the verbal emojis to turn your characters into more than just a paper dolls and emoticons. Use the verbal emojis to breathe dimension into your characters. Make your characters real people (again, or animals or other personified creations) with whom your readers can identify and emphasize. Use the verbal emojis to make your reader feel more than just:

Then, harness that "more" and mold it into something amazing. Use the verbal emojis to change the strength and severity of a feeling, change the orientation of a feeling, and even change the intensity of a scene or story.

Word
Word Play!
Play
Word Play!
Word
Play
Play

Word
Word Play!

119

Your Verbal Emojis at Work

We're jumping right to the wordplay on this one! Practice putting it all together and see how this little experiment has worked for you. We gave you the words (okay, and you supplied some, too). Now, it's time to PLAY: Create a passage that uses various positive, negative, and neutral words and phrases, used at different temperance levels, to develop a unique character. Consider your characterization practice and how the same verbal emoji can uniquely affect different scenes, especially when combined with the most powerful . . . and RIGHT . . . synonyms and upside-downed verbal emojis. Instead of a post, turn your character into a person.

As Promised . . .

*Overachievers, **IGNITE!** Yes, I know. Some of you really wanted more space for more verbal emojis and I promised I'd supply some lined and blank pages. Well, I can overachieve, too! I've also provided a couple of our standard tables in case you want to do some of your own defining, upside-downing, or categorizing for your verbal emojis additions!*

745. _____

746. _____

747. _____

748. _____

749. _____

750. _____

751. _____

752. _____

753. _____

754. _____

755. _____

756. _____

757. _____

758. _____

759. _____

760. _____

761. _____

762. _____

763. _____

764. _____

765. _____

766. _____

767. _____

768. _____

769. _____

770. _____

771. _____

772. _____

773. _____

774. _____

775. _____

776. _____

777. _____

778. _____

779. _____

780. _____

781. _____

782. _____

783. _____

784. _____

785. _____

786. _____

787. _____

788. _____

789. _____

790. _____

791. _____

792. _____

793. _____

794. _____

795. _____

796. _____

797. _____

798. _____

799. _____

800. _____

Alright, alright! That's enough, already! The next pages include:

- Blank 2-Column Tables
- Lined Note Pages
- Blank Note Pages

Afterword

Thanks for humoring us with the concept of verbal emojis. Verbal emojis seem to be slowly dying, and I'm glad you took at least a look through this Word Player's experiment. It's time to revive the verbal emojis and I hope we've done just that.

Really - people today are more familiar with emojis than adjectives. And it's a shame. Because the actual words can convey so much more than a yellow cartoon dot. Heck, one single verbal emoji can convey such complexity of emotion that you'd explode someone's phone sending the number of actual emojis necessary to do the work of a single verbal emoji.

Anyway, I hope you use this experimental book to build your stories strong.

But more than that, recall this book the next time you're asked "how are you?" And make a vow to answer honestly. Who cares of the asker doesn't really want to know. Who cares if your honest to goodness answer causes a blank stare or gaping mouth or the person to run in the other direction.

How am I? I'm freaking jubilant! How am I? Honestly, remorseful. How am I? Feeling kinda kinky actually - what of it? How am I? I'm damn explosive today, that's how I'm feeling - wanna take a couple steps back for me, yeah, thanks - best stay out of the line of fire on this one.

How am I today? Heck, I'm freaking jubilant and a bit remorseful but still feeling pretty kinky and damn explosive today - yeah, that's right - I'M A RAGING HORMONAL WOMAN TODAY AND YOU BETTER NOT CARE THAT"S WHAT'S UP!

....okay, so maybe that last bit is being a little too honest. And that would be a little weird depending on the setting. My coworkers would lock me in my office if I did that.

But really. No one is just "fine." Be more fun than "fine."

Resources Consulted

Online:
Merriam Webster Dictionary
Oxford English Dictionary
Urban Dictionary (Online)
Dictionary.com
Thesaurus.com
Roget's Thesaurus

Experientially:
The Plays We've Experienced
The Books We've Read
The Movies We've Seen
The Songs We've Heard
The Conversations We've OVERheard
The Relationships We've Entrusted

Cooperatively:
And Each Other

About the Authors

LAURA GREBE was born . . . arrived . . . was gifted to us on April 24th, 1985, her grandmother's namesake (oh! And Laura Holt from Remington Steele, too). Wife . . . spouse . . . betrothed . . . soulmate . . . other half to Josh Grebe and mother . . . mama . . . female parent . . . mommy . . . to Noah, the big brother Angel looking over his family from heaven, and Maddy, Noah's little sister.

A lifetime Wisconsinite and Patent Law lawyer living in the greater Milwaukee area, Laura knew she wanted to be a lawyer since the first grade when she started reading *Nancy Drew* books. She also loves science; reading (particularly mysteries with Nancy Drew and Sherlock Holmes being the favorites, science fiction, and tweeny-bopper mysteries and science fiction . . . um . . . *in German)*; scuba diving; jumping out of planes (attached to a qualified person wearing a parachute of course); baking cupcakes (aka: playing cupcake wars in my kitchen); showing Maddy the world; church; singing in the car (these days, usually to *Mickey Mouse Club, Dr. McStuffins, Sofia the First,* and *Bubble Guppies*), and spending way too much money on Zulily and Shutterfly.

Laura's *500+ Happenings to Prove Existence, 700+ Verbal Emojis,* and *1000+ Still Useful Words* were born out of her *Maternity Journal.* (Stay tuned! It's coming; we promise!) Through the unimaginable loss of a son that occurred before her pregnancy with Maddy, she and her husband, Josh, recognized the impossible relatability of journals to a grieving person who fearfully hopes and anticipates new life. Being often laid up during Maddy's prenatal days, Laura found herself digging deeper than ever to place intentional recognition on the things she did, felt, and observed. To Laura, these lists were tools to help her describe her days' experiences, but her publisher realized that, to the writers, and the therapeutic writing journalists they routinely work with, Laura's simple tools were anything but. So came the *Experimental Word Play* series that she now brings you.

She promises the venture into list-land won't change the uniqueness of her, punctuated by decided favorites that keep her connecting to the world and its words including: *animal* – bunny; *salty snack* - popcorn or Tostitos; *sweet snack* – cupcakes (we can't wait to bring you her *Cupcake Therapy* book!); *time of day* - morning sunrise; *season* – fall; *holiday* – Halloween; *color* - green (but not lime green, green green or olive green - more like leafy, natural green); *sport* – soccer; *dream vacation* – London; *drink* – iced tea; *clothing style* – classic, hippy, and/or old-school pin-up (you know, the kind that was sexy but didn't really show anything by today's standards); *music* – country; and *lucky number*– 13, which is how many favorites are listed here!

~~~~

Working with Laura to create the Experimental Word Play series was **REJI LABERJE**, Owner and Creative Director of Reji Laberje Writing and Publishing. Reji is a Bestselling Author with nineteen years of professional-level experience in the writing industry and her fortieth book hitting the presses in 2016. Laura's creativity was a joy for Reji to embrace. She looks forward to using the 500+, 700+, and 1000+ for the 20,000+ days she would be lucky to have left on God's green Earth. Also in that time, she intends to continue living life outside of Milwaukee with her husband of twenty years, Joe, and their active family of seven people and four pets.

Verbal Emojis

Verbal Emojis

Verbal Emojis

VERBAL

Emojis

Verbal

Emojis

VERBAL

EMOJIS

Made in the USA
Middletown, DE
26 October 2022

13491497R00080